bob

MANAGING PEOPLE GLOBALLY IS COMPLEX

Bob makes it easy

Watch a
3-minute **demo**

See how a people-first HCM enables global companies to thrive through change

PRAISE FOR *Present Company*

"I've been lucky to collaborate with Michael on numerous projects, and each one has been made substantially better by his presence. It feels like Michael has met the perfect scene partner in Timothy, and the tools they introduce in this fascinating new book are essential for successful collaboration, communication, and creation. This is a must-read for those looking to find joy in their journey and authenticity in their voice."

—ANTHONY VENEZIALE, cofounder of Speechless, Inc., and cocreator of Freestyle Love Supreme

"An inspiring and honest road map to high performance, *Present Company* is a blueprint designed to help anyone activate deeper presence at work and home. If you're looking to reach another level of connection, confidence, and creativity, this book will be your trusted guide. Timothy Dukes and Michael Landers combine their time-tested insights and compelling case studies in a way that makes high performance and deep presence attainable for anyone. *Present Company* dissects four powers of presence that could transform your life. If you're looking to increase your leadership capacity and become more intentional with your presence, this book is written for you."

—SHANE FELDMAN, CEO of Count Me In

"It is no longer sufficient for an organization to *succeed*. Boards of directors now recognize the negative financial impact of ineffective leadership, disengaged employees, and dysfunctional organizations. *Present Company* is aptly named because it offers the *gift* of authentic relationships and a healthy workplace that are proven to deliver significantly better results in every key measure of *success*. Read it. Apply it. Reap the benefits!"

—KIMBERLY WIEFLING, author of *Scrappy Project Management* and cofounder of Silicon Valley Alliances

"Within hours of reading Michael and Timothy's book, I was already putting their ideas and tools into practice: using the multitude of transitional moments during my day as thresholds to be more mindful of how I want to show up to my next meeting, interaction, or project. The realization that I waste so many of these opportunities makes me feel like someone just gave me more than twenty-four hours in a day. The assessments and tools for improving presence are eye-opening and powerful. If you're looking to live and work in a more intentional, effective, and rewarding way—both for you and the organizations you work for—this is a must-read!"

—JENNY EVANS, speaker, executive coach, and bestselling author of *The Resiliency rEvolution: Your Stress Solution for Life—60 Seconds at a Time*

"A real joy to read this book! Michael and Tim's ideas are insightful, practical, and absolutely relevant in these pivotal times. Their thorough understanding of different cultures and their fresh approach to shifting mindsets and behaviors through the art of presence are worth gold."

—FELIPE GOMEZ, global keynote speaker and author of *Attitude-E: The Method for Being Entrepreneurial and Fulfilling your Dreams*

"Timothy and Michael have combined their years of experience to create a lyrically written guide that encourages organizational leaders (and laypeople) to draw upon the deeper potential within their own life experience. *Present Company* provides the reader with the practical tools to build profoundly effective and nurturing relationships, teams, and organizations. I highly recommend it."

—MAJORA CARTER, real estate developer, urban revitalization strategist, and MacArthur Fellow

PRESENT COMPANY

PRESENT COMPANY

Cultivating Cultures of High Performance in Teams and Organizations

TIMOTHY
DUKES

MICHAEL
LANDERS

CONSCIOUS
CAPITALISM
PRESS™

Conscious Capitalism Press
www.consciouscapitalism.org/press

Round Table Companies
Packaging, production, and distribution services
www.roundtablecompanies.com
Deerfield, IL

Cover Design **Christy Bui**
Interior Design **Christy Bui, Sunny DiMartino**
Project Management **Keli McNeill**

Printed in the United States of America

First Edition: January 2021
10 9 8 7 6 5 4 3 2 1

Library of Congress Cataloging-in-Publication Data
Present company: cultivating cultures of high performance in teams and organizations
/ Timothy Dukes and Michael Landers.—1st ed. p. cm.
ISBN Hardcover: 978-1-950466-18-4
ISBN Paperback: 978-1-950466-17-7
ISBN Digital: 978-1-950466-19-1
Library of Congress Control Number: 2020915551

Conscious Capitalism Press is an imprint of Conscious Capitalism, Inc. The Conscious Capitalism Press logo is a trademark of Conscious Capitalism, Inc.

Round Table Companies and the RTC logo are trademarks of Writers of the Round Table, Inc.

Contents

A Straightforward Approach

I've been anticipating the arrival of this book for quite some time, and it couldn't have come at a more suitable moment. During an accelerated time of change, I have no doubt that *Present Company* will provide readers traction toward only one goal: the simple act of being present. I've learned from Dr. Dukes the power you can find when you're truly ready to reap the rewards of being present with your team, with your clients and customers, with your vendors and suppliers, and even with your family and friends.

The Four Powers of Presence detail a proven method of cultivating cultures of high integrity and performance. While not always easy to accomplish, this book has created a space for readers to grasp the true meaning of presence, as it relates to all facets of daily life. *Present Company* is a wake-up call for us to take hold of the here and now. After all, presence is really only about one person: you. You and your actions, your speech, and your intention.

Tim Dukes and Michael Landers lead by example by making their voices heard through this expertly written thought map.

Through *Present Company*, Dukes and Landers have redefined what it means to transition, occupy space, and *step into* dialogue.

I first became familiar with Dr. Dukes's work in 2013. We met over coffee, and we discussed the patterns we both saw in the world around us. In the time since, I have looked to Tim for his guidance and wisdom. His premise has always centered on the concept of presence, and this philosophical underpinning has been transformative, as I have negotiated both leadership and parental challenges, day in and day out.

Michael's work with crossing cultures requires a presence that is not always easy to inhabit. This he does well. As a multi-cultural maven, I take his work to heart.

As these two voices mesh, they interweave a rich contextual map for anyone looking to take themselves or the teams they lead toward personal and professional growth. This is one of my favorite quotes from the book: "Presence is the capacity to embrace our internal mental and emotional dynamics, while keeping us connected and related to the life surrounding us."

I expect this book to be a catalyst that creates the opportunity for you to be present and thus unlock more treasures in your life and in those whom your life touches.

Cheryl Contee
Inspirational Innovator | Social Impact Startup Pioneer | Sought-After Speaker and Author of the Amazon bestseller *Mechanical Bull: How You Can Achieve Startup Success*

Introduction

TIMOTHY

"Dr. Dukes, I made it . . . but now I don't know how to get out of it." More than six feet tall, in a wrinkled—but clearly expensive—grey suit, Robert appeared to have everything: a beachside home, a house in the city, and a senior position in a multinational organization. He was also fifty pounds overweight, exhausted, and alienated from his second wife and two young children. Professionally, Robert had become equally estranged from his executive team. He was isolated, depressed, and quickly losing track of his purpose.

While meeting with Robert, I understood that a standard rescue, resuscitate, and rehabilitate approach would require years of baby-step progress. I imagined myself in weekly meetings with this man, attempting to untangle the internal knots that had accumulated from years of high performance. Whether it was intentional or not, he had put his well-being and the well-being of others on hold as he rose to face the daily challenges of his career. He pushed through the natural limitations of his body and worked when he needed to rest. Preoccupied with the demands of his career, he missed the thousands of nuanced expressions on his children's faces: delight when the goldfish had babies, or

1

curiosity while exploring the progress of ants as they marched across the sidewalk on a sunny but cool fall morning. He abandoned his weekends by jumping online to handle a problem or even returning to his downtown office. While delving into the endless tasks that demanded attention, fueled by a desire to improve his performance, he began to forget. Almost without knowing it, moment to moment, day to day, he turned away from his relationships, his children, his physical health, and his passion for a balanced life. He was wealthy by traditional standards, yet he was approaching bankruptcy in body, mind, and spirit. To recover what he had forgotten would take an enormous commitment on his part. And it would take time.

It was in *this* moment, sitting in my office, at my large oak desk covered with papers, listening to Robert walk me through the latest argument with his wife, that I realized: I did not want to be sitting in that chair, in that office, guiding him through that arduous process. *There had to be a better way for leaders, for people, to be successful without paying such a high price.*

As a practicing psychotherapist who, for twenty years, saw more than twenty-five clients a week, I witnessed how helpful and life-changing the therapeutic process can be. But it is highly personalized and does not easily address the impact a client has on the lives of others. When we suffer, we create suffering for those around us. Of course, the opposite is also true: when we are well, we have a positive effect on the wellness of others.

I referred Robert to a very competent colleague and began my research. *I wanted to find a way to serve at the core of people's lives, while determining if it is possible to minimize the psychological, emotional, and physical price that high-functioning leaders pay for success.*

I wondered if a different approach might be more effective than psychotherapy: one in which people are as focused on their relationships as they are on themselves. I speculated that leadership works best when leaders build a culture in which people engage authentically. Relationships work best when they are reciprocal: when the focus is neither solely on oneself nor on the other person.

Of course, this thought didn't occur to me while sitting there in one session with a disheveled executive. It took months, perhaps years, to come to that realization. Eventually, I began to understand the importance of getting through to the individuals and leadership teams that steer organizations, to lower the cost of their success.

In the business context, I could witness such a decline in action. Working with clients like Robert was like watching a train wreck in slow motion: overwork as a result of miscommunication and unclear expectations, burnout that leads to poor decisions, avoidant behavior that stems from the inability or refusal to address and manage emotions. As a matter of fact, this refusal to feel is often at the core of many issues that leaders face. I speculated that by working with individuals within their community setting, I could help them learn how to make better decisions with their families, teams, and organizations—decisions that included their own wellness and wholeness—*before* their behavior damaged their lives.

There came a time when I made the move to rise out of my therapist chair and step into the conference room. What I did not know then was how challenging leaders and their executive teams could be. In the process of developing this understanding, I met Michael.

MICHAEL

When people ask me, "Michael, where are you from?" my quick answer is that I was born in Boston but raised overseas. The longer answer traces a journey from my birth in the United States to my childhood in Colombia, Brazil, and the Dominican Republic (with trips back to Boston every summer) to my early twenties in Japan before settling again in the United States.

Naturally, growing up in and living within these diverse populations informed my cultural perspective and also inspired the occasional identity crisis. When I am in Spanish-speaking countries in Latin America, I often say that I am *gringo* on the outside but *Latino* on the inside. My tendencies are a mash-up of the conditioning from these various cultures. Today, I happily identify with being a chameleon. I have developed a deep-rooted instinct to adapt as quickly as possible to the ways of the people around me.

Growing up this way plays an important role in my work, making me acutely aware of my cultural programming and that of others. Drawing from this diverse background and experience, I've created a set of cultural lenses that allow me to see the psychological, emotional, and behavioral patterns that leaders consciously or unconsciously foster in their teams and organizations. I recognize the norms that influence the culture of an organization.

Leadership is often displayed like fireworks: brilliant and impressive in the moment but quickly fading out of sight. The best ideas are often not lived out as the leader intended, and the inconsistencies between plans and behavior result in misinterpretation and miscommunication.

When I walk through the offices of growing start-ups or established companies, I see motivational signs like *GSD: Get Stuff Done* or *MSH: Make Stuff Happen* on conference room doors, and core values like *Be Accountable* and *Work Smart* plastered along the walls. I am cognizant that leaders usually have well-intentioned ideas influenced by core beliefs that may or may not have been thought out in great detail. When initially authentic and valuable symbols of the organization's intention and potential are left unattended, they start to fade like old photographs, settle like dust on a shelf.

Being authentic and sustaining your vision is a challenge. Remembering who you are, who you are willing to be, and who you *want* to be is a challenge. Keeping the symbols alive is a challenge. Many leaders are adept at bringing their teams or organizations to a certain degree of success, before finding that the impact of their leadership begins to stall. For many, this is the result of *working in your business* instead of *working on your business*. Often, the stress of the day-to-day grind incrementally detaches both leaders and team members from the larger vision and mission.

Driving toward outcomes at the expense of authentic connection with your teammates can damage the cultural context that is necessary for sustaining progress and productivity. Over time, you start to lose your grip on your intentions and may fail to recognize the slow erosion of the mechanics of working together; you forget about your team. The very values that account for your identity and your success fall by the wayside. Accountability turns into scapegoating and blame, inclusion becomes exclusion, and *Make Stuff Happen* turns into *CYA: Cover Your Ass*.

TIMOTHY AND MICHAEL

These concerns are what brought us together. We realized that we each carry a potent and well-developed commitment to helping leaders do better. We've worked with managers, directors, owners, founders, board members, CEOs, and executive teams. We've guided parents, mentors, coaches, spiritual leaders, and heads of foundations in both mission-driven and for-profit organizations.

In our combined years of lived and professional experience, we've learned that success depends on both presence and culture.

Presence ensures our awareness of what is active and operational in any given moment. The culture of your mind, your relationship, your family, or team is actually present. It reveals itself in every moment. If you are able to pay attention to your thoughts, feelings, and behaviors while also facilitating this consciousness with others, you can clearly see what works and what does not.

Let's begin with many of the dysfunctional realities we observe in teams and organizations. When allowed to persist, they drive failure. The following behaviors can cause conflict in any group, family unit, personal relationship, or team:

» Territorialism builds a tribal mentality and creates silos across business units and functions. One's perception of one's teammates can slowly degrade into the fear that they are competitors. Competition develops when, in fact, collaboration is the better choice.

» Fear of expressing one's voice is often legitimate given the unsafe environments that can, at times, develop in any organization. However, this fear becomes fertile ground for a *victim–persecutor* dynamic that, left unexamined, supports a corrosive team culture.

» Regression into past wounds, problematic patterns, and unhelpful storylines leads to failure when decisions are left on the table, agreements are broken, and trust is forgotten.

» Avoiding and masking the opportunity for productive conflict prevents development due to the rationale that the status quo or norm is better than taking this risk.

Presence is the antidote that stops these levers and triggers in their tracks. By showing up and doing the hard work of cultivating presence, leaders can expand their tolerance for listening deeply to the concerns and contributions of their team. When a culture of presence is cultivated, it serves the whole of the community:

» It unifies and aligns people, teams, and groups, while cultivating respect for collaborative leadership.
» It improves cross-sector communication and establishes constructive candor as a norm.
» It reduces insecurity and fears by developing a culture of mutual understanding.
» It clarifies the organizational norms that bring about success.
» It identifies problematic patterns and habits to establish thoughtful solutions.

The Partnership

Several years ago, we met through our mutual publicist, Andrea. This is what she wrote in an email:

I've been meaning to make this introduction for a long time now. I feel there is so much synergy between you, and it would simply be nuts for the two of you not to meet! You're both new authors, both consulting with some amazing companies and powerful decision-makers, and you're both quality gentlemen—kind, smart, funny guys. I have a strong feeling that you have a lot more in common than I even know.

Little did we realize how accurate Andrea's last sentence would be. From the moment we met, we began weaving a dialogue that brought us to where we are today: two very different professionals, with distinct but compatible career trajectories, who have aligned together for one common concern: *We are committed to supporting leaders to make better decisions in service of their teams, organizations, families, communities, and cultures.*

For organizations to grow, develop, and scale, people need to trust and depend on each other—both in the best of times and in the winds of sweeping change. A fundamental responsibility of a leader is to make sense of what is happening. On the surface, this seems pretty simple. However, the work involved requires understanding the influences that shape the dynamics, growth, and development of an organization. Leaders do not function successfully in isolation. They achieve success by building effective management teams and sustainable processes in support of successful behaviors that are able to thrive in an environment of persistent change. When challenges are too great, team members need to look to a leader to move them out of isolation, across any deep divide, and into a culture that supports their collaboration. Leaders cannot depend on the preexisting social systems, fueled by technology, to unite and keep their teams together. Using online messaging platforms to critique another team's progress has the potential to cause more problems than it solves. Texting your colleague about how you *feel* about a team meeting tends to split the culture into an *us-versus-them* mentality. Long emails about your point of view on the success or failure of the project creates unnecessary work for everyone on the email thread and strengthens the divide. Often, leaders realize that despite their best intentions, people begin to lose their connections with one another.

When leadership and social support is needed most, teams increasingly become more distant and isolated.

Individual leaders cannot establish and maintain a culture through self-determined action alone. A brilliant insight, a new vision, or any innovation inevitably disrupts the microecosystem of the team, organization, or family. This is not necessarily a problem, unless the disruption works against *homeostasis*— the balance of the variables that facilitates connection and cohesive equilibrium.

Robert, at the peak of his career, found himself too debilitated to continue. He was successful, but the net result of his success left him physically, emotionally, relationally, and spiritually exhausted. *His success* also exacted a price from others. As he damaged and lost significant connections in his life, he found himself isolated and alone. His growing problems had become impossible to ignore and began to surface in ways that were very difficult to face and resolve. *What we refuse to acknowledge today, we inherit tomorrow.*

Isolated trees have a shorter life expectancy than those connected to a forest or larger ecosystem. It takes a forest to create a microclimate that is suitable for the growth of an individual tree. Similarly, it takes a collective to create the culture and microclimate suitable for the growth and sustenance of an individual leader, the team, and the organization. Like a forest, an organization will thrive due to an embedded system, which recognizes the significance of the interconnections of its people. This is what creates and sustains culture. A leader cannot establish a consistent and cohesive team climate or ecosystem on his or her own.

Individual, team, and organizational growth and development depends upon collective effort—working together as a whole, as a culture. This is the responsibility of every team member. Individuals work to cultivate this culture by sticking to the task of building and maintaining cohesive connections, while refusing to allow themselves or their teammates to become isolated, displaced, or ineffective. No matter the context, people need one another to develop and sustain success. As a leader, you are interdependent with the people in your life. The cultivation of a sustainable culture is forged through your ability and willingness to *show up, engage,* and *be present.* Without presence, an authentic social network may never form. You may find yourself participating in a false world of your own making, an incidental culture, one that seems to exist due to an accidental give-and-take rather than consistent moment-to-moment determination. With presence, you have the option to choose.

Additionally, as a member of the team, do you allow your leaders to function in a way that is suboptimal and counterproductive? Or do you insist that the culture allows your full participation and integration into the team? This book, *Present Company,* explores the tools and methods necessary to cultivate a culture of true presence. It highlights the obstacles you knowingly and unknowingly place in your way. *Presence* is not an isolated act or concept that can be superimposed on a situation. It is the result of an ongoing process of authentic exchanges between you and the relationships you have with others.

The pages that follow invite you to explore the process of how to cultivate a sustainable culture of high performance through your ability and willingness to show up and be present. A culture without intention and presence creates disconnection. A cultivated culture, one with intentional and conscious involvement among its people, evolves out of lived experience that is repeated in present time. In this present social construct, there is an opportunity to consciously participate in a joint network, a world beyond anything you can generate by yourself. Through active dialogue—both spoken and unspoken—you can establish and continue to develop a robust and intelligent foundation for your humanity.

Together with others, you can participate in consciously shifting the systems from something you maintain to something that serves everyone involved.

On Presence

Typically, it is assumed that if we focus on one thing, we are being present. Often, we associate presence with our ability to concentrate—to apply our attention to a single point and keep it there. You might be at the dinner table, a family member is talking about their day, and you are listening. You are present, aren't you? Or perhaps you're in a meeting. You are in charge of the agenda and things seem to be going according to schedule. That's being present, right? To a certain degree, yes—but what if we shift the paradigm a bit?

Rewind and go back to the dinner table. Your family member is speaking. You hear her words, and as the story unfolds, you notice the movement of her lips, the light in her eyes, the excited rhythm of her breath. At the same time, you are aware of how you feel, the joy in your heart, as you notice how the climate or tonal quality of the entire family resonates with her story. You are also aware of the competing demands for your thinking: some unfinished piece of business, the waiting emails, a project deadline on the horizon. True presence includes an open and receptive attitude that allows for a flow of sensory awareness that rounds your experience into wholeness. In this dynamic consciousness, in spite of the competing distractions, you recognize your capacity for receptive awareness, sustaining a relational environment. Perhaps you are all laughing at something, you exchange smiles, you feel close, and you hold other demands for your attention at bay, so as not to dislocate yourself from your family. And you know there will be a time, in the near future, where you can address your business concerns.

Familiar? I am sure it is. We are now beginning to enter the unfolding nature of moment-to-moment presence. Presence is the result of the exchange that reveals our fundamental connectedness, while being inclusive of the distractions that pull us from these connections. Presence is the capacity to embrace our internal mental and emotional dynamics, while keeping us connected and related to the life surrounding us.

Consider Ted, the CEO of a booming start-up recently acquired by a much larger firm. He knows how to lead. Reserved, thorough, and mindful, he enters an all-hands meeting cradling a cup of coffee. Cell phone intentionally left behind, his assistant knows to never disturb him, unless there is a family emergency. Ted stands to the side, listening, observing, and attuning himself to the situation. He closely follows the energy in the room as it builds.

When he feels the time is right, he inserts himself into the conversation. Keen to add value, determined to be efficient, willing to balance conflicting needs, Ted's words are measured and authentic, informed by the agenda of the other leaders. His participation enhances the current dynamics. If necessary, his actions and words disrupt the process to support a change in direction or a deepening of dialogue. Much like the conductor of an orchestra, Ted's job is to harmonize, while ensuring that the meeting is well orchestrated, intended results are achieved, and that the meeting is brought to an artistic conclusion.

The best leaders realize that they are not a one-person act. As they consciously attend to their thoughts and feelings, they are informed by the thoughts and feelings of those in the room. They attune themselves empathically. A reciprocal engagement unfolds when leaders realize that just as they act unto others, they have the potential to be acted upon. In every moment, they are aware that they are both the observer and the observed. In this sense, presence is an exchange that is additive, not extractive. The present leader's behavior enhances the conditions in the room, supporting a process where there is a give-and-take of consideration and energy.

As Ted offers his awareness and attention, he allows the group consciousness to inform him—the process becomes codetermined. The act of opening this capacity moves him from a unilateral orientation, *this is how it is done*, to multilateral realizations, *we are all in this together*. Ted is present in a culture that he is largely responsible for cultivating.

Through conscious intention, you have a choice to give your awareness to whatever is within your field of attention. You can then choose to support and amplify its existence. When you interact in the moment, you are both affecting and being affected by the situation. As you achieve clarity, you also invite into consciousness the next thing to be clarified. Like a light attracting a moth, presence pulls and nourishes the moment into a more dynamic, inclusive, and additive exchange. Without presence, you are sorely missing out on the positive interaction you can have with yourself, those around you, and even your surroundings. When your family, team, or community makes the mutual decision to maintain presence, a third thing—a field of exchange, the relationship—emerges. It is here that the culture of presence develops and takes root.

Without this intentional, dynamic engagement, our relational moments are simply an interaction between self and other, on and off, good and bad, inner and outer. Presence hinges on our determination to be conscious of how we affect the world around us, while at the same time deepening our awareness of how the world affects us.

The Four Powers of Presence

Over the years, we have been engaged—both together and independently—by prominent executives and by team leaders seeking change. These clients have been searching for sustained high performance for themselves and for their teams. As a result of our work, we have become, in many instances, witnesses to internal cultural shifts. When successful in helping our clients, we observe individuals and teams engaging mindfully when transitioning between team meetings and other interactions. We notice that people are attentive to their impact upon one another, recognizing how they are feeling in a given moment. We marvel at teams who choose vulnerability over masking or deflecting. And we easily detect when true multilateral connections exist among teammates. Presence is activated by four specific cultivated abilities or behaviors that, when combined, establish a cultivated ecosystem, a Culture of Presence.

This chapter introduces the Four Powers of Presence: Induction, Awareness, Authenticity, and Connection. When orchestrated empathetically, these specific abilities allow a culture of presence to emerge. Each power has its own characteristics.

When individually cultivated, they bring you value in your roles both as leader and team member. However, when brought together as a unified and determined choice, they can take you to an expanded degree of success. We will explore how the powers cycle and flow, while highlighting the influence they have on families, teams, and organizations as a whole. Specifically, we will highlight where each power comes from, how to access it, and how it can have an impact on the individual and on the community.

The Power of Induction

An *induction* is an invitation, a request, or a compelling demand to join and participate in something outside of yourself. It is an opportunity to shift your thinking and feelings. As you participate in a social context, you can experience yourself having been inducted into the event or group. With those you live with, you are inducted into the climate or the feel of your home. Induction is an invitation to shift your awareness, as you return to your partner, child, pet, or the simple peace of your environment. At the gym, you are inducted, as you enter into the flow of the atmosphere of fitness. In your church, temple, or synagogue, you are in the proximity of spiritual and religious ceremony, as you are potentially inducted into the sacred. In nature, you are inducted into the potential to resonate with the dynamic life of the natural world. In business, induction is an open invitation from a leader to work authentically with their team.

For the most part, people participate consistently from one situation, event, or meeting to the next. You depend on yourself to be consistent and comfortable with how you are, as well as how you are perceived. Whether it is a one-on-one exchange, a team meeting, or an all-hands affair, the induction is a profound, yet simple, invitation for all to enter, connect, and proceed, regardless of the space. This is an invitation to move out of the comfort of the norm and into the interdependent and vibrant possibility of authentic engagement.

Induction disrupts the norm and sets *possibility* into *action*. You can do this whenever you *join* with another person, moving from separate to together, from me to you, you to me, and settling on a place we call *us*. This conscious intention supports a transition from your individual experience to a context where meaning is developed as a collective reality. You induce mutual collaboration. You move the team, the family, the community into a collaborating microclimate. As you begin to experience the others and they experience you, you move your awareness, thinking, and behavior to be inclusive, out of separation and isolation and into an experience that generates new potential.

Think for a moment of how you go about your days. You enter team meetings, have a call with a customer, commute, take a break, eat lunch, step from a work dynamic into the family or friend dynamic. All of these daily occurrences tend to happen without your paying close attention to the transitional moments. You are often too focused on what just happened or on your expectations of what will happen next. The space between moments seems to have lost value. Without a clear return on the investment of time and effort made, you often misperceive these moments as useless or wasted and pass through them unattuned. The Power of Induction is the necessary attunement that allows you to pay attention to those transitional moments to regulate yourself and others. In other words, the life that was there before you arrived is intact, as it consciously informs you of what is happening and of what is about to happen.

The Power of Awareness

What are you aware of in this moment? Perhaps there is a tension in your hands, your breath shallow, a slight itch on your nose? What about your eyes? Clear as day? Slightly blurred? Consciousness arises when you become aware of the object of your perception and allow your mind and senses to register the experience. For many of us, awareness is generally thought of as an individual's ability to pay attention. However, as I am aware of you, I must recognize that you are potentially aware of me. As I perceive you, you perceive me. I must also allow for the possibility that our perceptions are not the same. The power of awareness allows for this simultaneous recognition of our mutual perceptions and our potential impact upon one another.

The Power of Authenticity

What is authenticity all about? Being vulnerable and choosing to leave one's flaws exposed. These flaws could be as simple as showing annoyance or anger at someone's remark, instead of masking it with deflection or denial. Authenticity allows for a true acknowledgment of the feeling and perhaps the reasoning behind it. When you are open to being perceived as you are, as you reveal yourself, vulnerability is the inevitable outcome. Authenticity is the willingness to feel what you need to feel to show up and be revealed as you are and to know that as you are revealed, you are also seen by others.

This power of authenticity is forged in a willingness to be both created and destroyed by how others perceive you. Authenticity emerges as you return to the moment as you are and as you have been impacted by the previous moment. Misunderstandings occur when there is discord between your intentions and how you are perceived. When you are authentically engaged in the present moment, your authenticity is not a fixed or static position. It emerges, iteration after iteration, as you fashion and are fashioned in this moment and the next.

The Power of Connection

"I enjoy working with you. You get it."

"Working with you is easy. No need to explain things: we just flow."

"I love being a customer here. They just know how to treat you right."

When engaged, people understand your intention and recognize your preferences, expectations, and work style. In many cases, the other person may have similar philosophies. There is ease because you don't have to spend time explaining or defining what things mean; people just get it. They get you, your culture, and your way of being. These connections have the potential to build strong, long-lasting friendships. At work, they often lead to preferential treatment, better opportunities for visibility, and a clear path to promotion.

On the flip side, when you encounter people who don't seem to *get it*, you can feel uncomfortable, perplexed, and frustrated. You may shut down, burst with emotion, or give up and walk away—ultimately missing opportunities to build positive connections. Culture clashes breed alienation, bias, and exclusion. At work, they lead to *us-versus-them* mentalities, competition over collaboration, lowered retention and productivity, and a culture of silence, denial, and avoidance.

When true two-way bonds are formed, you have accessed the Power of Connection. Often, these connections happen quite randomly, but we all have the potential to ensure that these bonds are formed more regularly. You can choose to connect or intentionally allow others to connect with you. Think about your current relationships at work and in your personal life. How many authentic connections do you have? Would you like to form more?

When you don't connect as you think you should or would like to, an opportunity presents itself. The opportunity is to stop and connect to what is occurring in your experience, just as it is. Let the moment imprint itself on you. And if you do not land where you had hoped to have landed, you can do something about it.

Continuity and Present Company

Once true reciprocal connections are made, a leader's challenge becomes one of sustainability. How do you ensure that what you have created—*authentic presence*—will remain once you are no longer connected physically or virtually? What will allow for that next moment, that next meeting, to retain what has been so mindfully cultivated?

Sustaining presence is rooted in how you handle the transitions that fill your days. In our work, we have found that transitions are one of the greatest sources of stress for leaders and for organizations. The pace of today's technological existence allows for little to no transition time from one moment or activity to the next: call to call, meeting to meeting, home to car, car to home. You are constantly moving without allowing the time and space to acknowledge what you are leaving and what you are entering.

The lack of recognition of the importance of transitions creates an unintended impact on you, your family, friends, partners, colleagues, clients, and community. Without mindful transitions, you risk carrying the residue of every previous encounter into the next. Presence ensures that the myriad shifts are acknowledged, so that the next opportunity is primed to flourish.

The Cycle

When orchestrated, the Four Powers of Presence act to establish an ecosystem, a Culture of Presence. In the flow of continuity,

Induction + Awareness + Authenticity + Connection
= **Presence.**

Induction creates the space for personal and interpersonal **awareness**. In turn, as you shift outside of the familiar patterns of thinking and behavior, there is a possibility that you may become more open and vulnerable, for the sake of **authenticity**. Your openness creates the right environment for the formation of authentic **connections**. These connections ensure the likelihood of a sustainable continuity, enabling the next cycle to begin.

When the Four Powers unite, the presence that emerges is a powerful dynamic. In these moments, you will be greeted with change and the unfolding opportunity to embrace and be embraced by the next moment. Between each moment and the next, there is the transitional dynamic that can inhibit continuity. When you notice that the flow dissipates, come back and begin again. Since this is much easier said than done, we will highlight specific challenges that may arise when moving from one power to the next—in particular, the unintended results that can occur when one or more of the powers may not yet be present.

For example, when Induction is missing, the result is one of Limited Sustainability as illustrated in the equation:

~~Induction~~ + Awareness + Authenticity + Connection
= Limited Sustainability

Without Induction in our equation, there is no guarantee that you or those you engage with will be able to transition in a way that is unencumbered from your previous encounters. When it comes to a lack of awareness, the equation looks like this:

Induction + ~~Awareness~~ + Authenticity + Connection
= Diminished Potential

Without a balanced awareness of self, the other, and the relationship, a one-sided vision is left to dictate the process, potentially limiting the opportunity for growth.

As you orchestrate the Four Powers of Presence, you establish an ecosystem, a Culture of Presence:

Induction + Awareness + Authenticity + Connection
= Presence.

The Power of
Induction

MICHAEL

R ecently, I hired a painter to refinish the ceiling and walls
of my daughter's bedroom. Think about this painter's process: she needed to establish the *who*, *what*, *when*, and *how* of
the project. First, the *who*. She needed to meet me, her client,
and initiate the dynamics of our collaboration. Second, she had
to understand my expectations, so we could come to an agreement about *what* the finished product would look like. The *when*
involved setting deadlines and aligning our mutual schedules.
Then for the *how*. How would she approach the project? She
needed to consider isolating the room from the rest of the house,
because change can be messy—especially when it involves sand-
paper, dust, and paint. Next, she had to protect the surfaces that
would not be involved: the floor was to be covered, the ceiling to
be taped. The woodwork and the walls would require different
treatments (surfaces sanded, cracks and holes filled). Finally,

she had to be confident that she had the skill, energy, and determination to complete the project. To ensure a successful outcome, the painter needed to consider all of this before her first brush stroke.

This preparation is an act of induction. It begins the process. Without thorough preparation, the walls may be left with an uneven finish or the paint could crack and peel over time. It would *look* like a rushed job, because it would have *been* a rush job.

This preparatory process is the experience of recognizing that your impulse, idea, or solution may not be ready to be presented to the world. This means that you check yourself, incubate what is trying to happen, and wait a little bit longer before you act. Master painters know when their creation is ready to be shared with the world. Until that time, they continue to develop their work and *turn it to the wall* until the time is right and the painting is ready to reveal itself. It could be the email that sits in the draft folder a bit longer, or the feedback you wait some time to give, or even an initial reaction that you choose to stifle until you can process things a bit longer.

Without induction—the intentional preparation for the job ahead—a desirable outcome is difficult to achieve. Without induction, you have unintended, and often undesirable, results.

You experience induction all the time. It is the moment just before the tap of the conductor's baton and the last few steps into a stadium before you catch a glimpse of the playing field. It is the feeling when the lights go down and you see the shadowy musicians take up their instruments. It is the slight jolt of a plane as the thrusters kick in and, suddenly, you are on your way.

Induction is the thing that fills your lungs with the air of excited anticipation. It makes you close your eyes and see into what is coming next; it brings a crowd of strangers together to share a single focus. These moments immerse you in presence and offer an opportunity to carry that presence with you into this moment and the next. It is why these events are so memorable, because you are fully present.

Finding yourself in the present moment is not just powerful—it is a power that you can cultivate. Induction sets the context, foundation, and frame that holds you in this moment. It keeps you tethered and prepared for what is next. It primes you to transition into an intentional state of mind, in which you consciously choose to participate. This choice moves you over the threshold from isolated to integrated. It is an invitation to join the ceremony, paving the way for a deeper level of engagement. It is *induction*.

The Wake You Make

Imagine you are running late to a meeting. It's a familiar feeling: the momentum of the morning has gotten away from you. Whether or not it was your fault, you are now stewing in the anxiety and frustration of a morning gone awry. From the frenetic pace of your commute to the rushed (or altogether neglected) greetings as you enter the office, these behaviors color how you feel. And these feelings condition how you act and how you are perceived.

Without a conscious induction, you unconsciously carry this effect—your display of feelings—into the meeting, communicated through gestures, facial expressions, body postures, tone, and the volume of your voice. You cannot know what processes are going to be interrupted or opportunities unrealized because you did not take the time to transition from your state of mind before you arrived to the state of mind that would have allowed you to integrate into that process. As you enter the meeting, you create a wake of unintended and unconscious consequences. Your attitude ripples in waves. You are neither conscious of your intention nor of the potential results of your actions. You did not toss a pebble into the group process but rather a boulder. Yes, a boulder, heaved right into the center of the pond—the team's process.

When we are working with leaders and see this happen, we often ask them, *Was it your intention to create such a splash that the frogs should end up in the trees?* Their response is usually, *Trees? Frogs? What in the world are you talking about?*

We explain further. Every room you enter is an ecosystem. This meeting is the pond and your team members are the frogs and other critters living in its environment. Did you notice them before you decided to heave yourself—a boulder—into the water? They were thriving in their habitat—calm, working together, attentive to one another in their shared space. Instead of assessing this and adjusting to align *with* the ecosystem, you caused an act of disruption. Now, forced to flee the comfortable cohabitation of the pond, the frogs have leapt for the trees. And they will stay there, isolated around the perimeter of the moment, until the ripples diffuse and the waters of their environment resettle. Before they even consider the possibility of returning to engage authentically, they will anxiously wait to see what happens next. Often, they do not move out of their retreat, participating from a distant and dislocated posture, for the remainder of the meeting.

Personal motivation may be your focus: *I want to make a sale. I want to build trust. I want to motivate my team, demonstrate credibility, or increase efficiency.* These are common desires. We all want to feel the support and approval of our peers. As you move through your day, you can't help but create some sort of wake in every single interaction. Canceling a meeting, reprimanding a colleague, laughing at a mishap, looking at your phone—all of these behaviors have an impact. As a leader, employee, parent, partner, or peer, are you aware of how your conscious and unconscious actions ripple into your relationships and environment? Are you aware of the wake you make?

What Is Hidden?

Imagine you are walking through a forest. What do you notice? Is the ground hard? Or is it soft from recent rain or layers of fallen leaves? Are there rocks and roots to navigate? Are you leaving footprints in the mud? How do your footprints affect the forest floor? Do they create a new terrain for bugs to crawl upon? Do they dry, harden, and leave a mark? Do they gather water?

One thing is certain: you have imprinted yourself into the forest and it has also had an effect on you.

TIM

Recently, my friend John and I were walking in an old-growth redwood forest. It was quiet, almost too quiet. John whispered, "You know, the life that was here before we arrived will not return for perhaps an hour after we have gone." Curious, I asked what he meant. He replied, "When I return to Minnesota and we go hunting, as we enter the forest, our intrusion causes most of the animals to disappear. It is as though they know our intention. However, if we are able to remain still and quiet our minds, the life that is hidden eventually forgets that we are there and returns."

Later, while reflecting on John's wisdom, I began to notice the similarities between the ecosystem of the forest and the ecosystem of the office. Like the creatures in the woods, a group of employees and coworkers will remain withdrawn or hidden if their leader fails to integrate safely and participate authentically. In the disrupted office environment, the displaced individuals want to and need to return to business as usual, but they will linger uncomfortably in the shadows at the periphery until the environment returns to a safe and stable equilibrium. And that may not happen until the leader has left the premises.

As a leader, what do you do to support seamless value creation rather than negative disruption? How do you do a better job of understanding what already exists in those moments just before you arrive? How do you recognize the threshold that you are about to step through? How do you include yourself, so that your participation is integrative, not disruptive—or, worse, exploitative? Could it be a leader's responsibility to facilitate this collaborative ecology?

When you enter an existing environment (whether it's an ongoing meeting or just a new day at the office), it is your responsibility to recognize that your unattuned intrusion has the potential to subjugate, ostracize, or disallow what was there before you arrived. Rather than crashing onto the scene with big, bossy footsteps, leaders who use induction align themselves with the atmosphere and energy of the team. This thoughtful approach allows the team to risk staying present and engaged and resume their intersubjective functions, now with the leader included.

By paying attention to transitional moments, you can attune yourself to the appropriate frequency of that particular situation. By scaling or regulating yourself, the existing atmosphere can remain intact. You can develop the empathic awareness, sensitivity, and skill to fully integrate into the moment and remain present. This choice cultivates a culture that allows for those who are hidden to reappear, those who are silenced to be listened to, and those who are forgotten to be recognized. And this is where the true value of a team is appreciated—when all of its voices are heard.

The power of induction initially establishes this attunement, which can prevent you from reducing or damaging the cultural context in unintended ways. All of us have the full capacity to uncover this power in our daily lives. We just have to consciously choose to use it.

Now Is the Time

Over the course of any given day, there are hundreds of opportunities to use the power of induction. In fact, you probably do so without knowing. Think back to a time when you were highly aware of the transition between one moment and the next, and consider what was revealed. Perhaps it was before an important meeting or presentation or maybe a highly anticipated show or a sports event. Induction can be practiced in simple ways. For some, eating a meal is something they take for granted. Food is put in front of us and we eat. For others, they take a moment to say "thank you" or offer a toast. These intentions prime us to be present for what is about to happen.

Typically, in Japan, when someone returns to a home or place of work, they will say "tadaima" as they cross the threshold. In response, the people who are present will call out "okaerinasai." Simply put, "tadaima" means "I have returned," and "okaerinasai" means "welcome back or welcome home." These statements are deeply ingrained at all levels in Japanese society. They are some of the earliest words that children speak. They highlight the transitional moment and reinforce the concept of group harmony.

In a subtle way, these simple words say, "I am with you." They make individual comings and goings a communal act.

Take a moment to think about this. By authentically announcing that you are present, you can ignite and bring to life your family gathering, a team meeting, or a community get-together. As you reveal yourself into the moment, the others reveal themselves to you and to one another. This is pretty straightforward, yet it is a powerful use of your time, energy, and consideration.

Now compare this to your typical day, either at home or in the office. How often does your day unfold without your paying attention to the transitional experience? You are too preoccupied with the past or your expectations of the future. Perhaps you are not focused enough. The space between moments, between breaths, seems to have lost value. You move along from one activity to the next with little distinction and appreciation of the potent possibility that each moment holds.

Many of us normalize this vague disconnect and adapt to being in proximity to one another without authentically engaging. You may do this for no apparent reason other than that you are merely not paying attention. You may not be aware of either the immediate impact or the residual detachment that you foster. Unfortunately, many of us unconsciously participate in the unfolding reality with a sense of *this is just how it is*. However, to prosper, your relationship with yourself and with others requires you to continually update and stay connected to the depth and breadth of your experience.

When team members go into a meeting without fully transitioning into the context of the moment, safety and participation is individually assessed and determined. It is every man or woman for themselves. Each person is left to their respective capacity to join the meeting. One member could be distracted by an exchange that they had before the meeting. Another could be focused on their personal agenda, with a determination to force it into this meeting. Some may be feeling unresolved animosity toward a coworker, while others may be grappling with turmoil at home. Team members may even be experiencing harassment or marginalization due to their race or gender. Around the room, these individual experiences silently inform and have an effect on the experience of the whole.

When you consciously enter a meeting, can you set aside your individual problems and focus on the greater good? Does a conscious entering allow you to be sympathetic to others who may be entering with challenges? Does consciously starting a meeting do something else entirely and open everyone up to unexpected possibility?

Without clarity and conscious intention, dysfunction can be normalized. These individual concerns may be a one-time consideration or the result of patterning; either one becomes an obstacle to full participation. If the meeting proceeds with these freewheeling, individual encumbrances, the likelihood of a successful team outcome reduces dramatically. For many teams, this individualistic mentality can lead to a culture where people contribute less authentically, activate unwanted patterns, perceive threats more readily, and make obstacles the norm. In this culture of nonpresence, people stick to their individual positions instead of recognizing the greater opportunities to be found in authentic connection.

How to Activate Induction

At any given moment, induction is activated by learning to recognize intention—both your own and the intentions of those around you. To transition through the thresholds that often keep people separated, it is important to establish a resonant awareness and to attune empathically to the others in the room and to the culture of the group. Although induction begins on an individual level, it must be cultivated by the community to reverberate into the larger culture.

When you cross the gap between your experience of certainty and the introduction of what is next, you have the opportunity to bring awareness to the threshold of this experience. This is something you experience all day, every day.

Try to focus on the experience when you move from this to that: when you get out of bed, enter the shower, dress for the day, leave your home, step into the car or onto the bus. Every transition offers the opportunity to practice. To cross a threshold provides the opportunity to unite yourself with the next dynamic in the cycle of presence.

Every moment is in preparation for the transition to the next moment. With this awareness, your ability to make wise transitions will increase. Change will then become an ally, not the enemy.

The following section explores advice and guidelines for activating induction—for both an individual and a team.

Self-Induction

As an individual, especially as a leader, you have the potential to initiate change through your actions, behaviors, even your thoughts. A chain reaction can begin with a simple decision: to be present and intentional in the moment-to-moment progression of the day.

Comings and Goings

Whether your commute includes a forty-five-minute train ride, a five-minute walk, or a few steps into your home office, the act of induction begins well before you enter the workplace. Unfortunately, this crucial time often devolves into a complacent, sleepy routine or a chaotic scramble to get out of the door. By maintaining conscious intention, by recognizing the threshold, these intervals can be reclaimed and functional ceremonies established.

Getting ready: Whether you are the type of person who primps for hours or who rolls out the door in fifteen minutes, getting dressed can be an opportunity to think about who you want to be today and how you want to present yourself to the world. Even if your wardrobe is just a simple suit, a sweater, or a mandatory uniform, this time allows you to mentally step into the authentic self that you intend to express throughout the day. The practice isn't limited to your external appearance. Other morning rituals can be used to set your internal compass toward intention. Do you go out for an early-morning walk to engage with and appreciate nature? Do you make the perfect smoothie or cup of coffee to sustain yourself for the hard work ahead? Do you take a moment to play with a pet or hug a loved one to fill your internal capacity for gratitude and affection? These small steps can translate into powerful moments of induction.

Commuting: Getting to work presents an opportunity to prepare and practice how you will engage with others in your environment. Whether you are navigating around other drivers on the road or crammed in close proximity to others on public transportation, you can make a conscious decision about how you operate in relation to the lives around you. This doesn't necessarily mean striking up a conversation with the tired stranger on the subway. Instead, try to be conscious of the small thoughts and gestures that make a big contribution to a shared environment. Giving someone the right-of-way or a smile can set the tone for how you will interact with other strangers, peers, and colleagues throughout the day.

Stepping into the workplace: Recognize the actions you intend to take for the first thirty minutes and, by this, set a foundation for a successful day. Recognize each and every threshold that demarcates the transitions in your day. Develop a series of actions to strengthen the practice. What is their sequence? How does each step contribute to setting the overall tone for the day? My list often includes: 1. Drink a glass of water and fill my water bottle. 2. Make a brief and authentic connection with at least three people. 3. Clean and order my work environment. 4. Flag my emails for deletion, delegation, or to-dos. 5. Get that cup of coffee on my desk. 6. Stop for three minutes, rest in the moment, breathe and catch up. 7. Shift into the mindset of productivity and get busy.

Departures: Whether you are stepping out of the office for a private meeting or heading home at the end of the day, departures are an equally important moment of transition for you and those around you. As you begin to think about what is next—your agenda for a working lunch or the mountain of laundry waiting at home—take a moment to acknowledge and appreciate that you are transitioning out of your current environment. Note what you have accomplished. Determine what to leave behind, pick up later in the evening, or put off until the following day. Take a physical or mental note, so that what you are letting go of can be easily accessed down the road.

High-performance individuals all have one thing in common: they will step away from their endeavor when they are at peak, or close to peak, performance. A writer will build out the narrative to where it is alive and flowing, write a little bit more, then step away. She feels that when she returns, she will pick up where she left off. Long-distance runners will train to peak and finish the run with the expectation that when they return, they will start here and build to the next level. Communicators will often conclude a conversation or a meeting when the energy is most vibrant. My uncle used to say, "When you leave someone, leave them happy and laughing. They will always look forward to the next time."

Returning home: Before you walk in the door, consider ways that you can adjust and attune yourself to the upcoming environment. Note the threshold. Are there small accommodations that you can make to set your expectations and align yourself with who or what is to come? Develop your own transition ceremonies to initiate induction. Take three deep breaths and consider the differences between where you were and where you are now. Think about the people you will be joining and what they have gone through since you were last together. Before you arrive, send a simple text message or make a phone call to check in and set their expectations. Take stock of your mood or temperament—how available are you to being greeted? How do you want to spend the evening? How can you make sure those goals are shared and achieved? Your conscious intentions and a few rituals can help bridge the gap and make certain that your return is a success for all.

Going to sleep: At the end of the day, preparing for sleep is probably one of the most valuable transitions you make. It is as important as preparing for the day. The induction into sleep has the potential to transition you from your day of activity to a night of deep rest.

Here are a few guidelines. Make sure that the bedroom is clean, uncluttered, and comfortable. Consider a bath or shower to cleanse away the physical and emotional vestiges of the day. Make sure that your clothing and bedding are comfortable and that they breathe easily. Give yourself enough time away from electronics and screens, so that you fully leave those stimuli behind. Make sure that the room is dark. Take a moment to recount the day; reflect on three learnings. Find one thing you may do differently tomorrow. Set your intention to dream and to deeply rest.

Mood and the Moment

Induction is about being malleable and adapting your mood to the moment. Can you establish your own ceremonies to practice induction for one day, for several days, a week?

Conversations and collaborations: Meetings and conversations are a critical context for induction in the workplace. Whether they are *actual* or *virtual*, they put you in front of other people. You are in real time and actually in relationship. What is your particular way of making these transitions? Do you take this opportunity to recognize the threshold, as you move from one experience to the other?

Meeting one-on-one: Take a moment to reflect on the expectations of the other person you are meeting, before you have the meeting. Consider your goals and agenda, but also try to imagine their intention. What are they anticipating? Try to recall your most recent conversation: What has transpired since your previous connection? How can you build on that and maintain cohesion and continuity? How might your thoughts and feelings affect the dynamics of the encounter? Notice that as you prepare for the meeting, you are shifting your mood and your frame of mind.

Meeting with your team: Take a moment and pause, be clear where you are coming from and where you are going. Recognize what you want to give to and receive from this meeting. This shifts your intention and resets your expectations. This meeting is the next context in which your team will manifest. It has a living history. There is always the present moment, which needs to be consistently occupied. The team has a future that it will be living into. As with any other entity, for it to thrive it deserves (even requires) your care and consideration.

All-hands meeting: Take a moment to envision what the attendees may have experienced since the last meeting. Were expectations addressed, agreements kept, goals met? What is the undercurrent of how they may feel as a result? Success? Anxiety? Fear? Excitement? Boredom? Anger? Engagement? Attune yourself to the emotional, psychological, and behavioral climate. The all-hands meeting is a moment when many, if not all, of the organization's contributors gather. It is an optimal opportunity to listen, connect, broaden, and deepen the vision and the mission. It is a time to clarify goals, milestones, successes as well as the challenges ahead. Every word and behavior emanating from the leadership team has the potential to enhance and shape the meeting's success.

Meeting for lunch: Consider your presence. How will it impact the person you are with? Explore the reason for the meeting. Is it a working lunch? Is it a time for camaraderie? An influencing opportunity? How will you deepen your rapport? How will you manage the pace, the flow of conversation? Will you recognize if there is an equal measure of you, of the others, and of the relationship? Remember to engage, broaden, and deepen your connection.

Meeting a client: When you think about it, having a client who values what you have to offer is a privilege. Do you have your way of acknowledging this? Think for a moment about what this meeting is about. Essentially, you are meeting to set yourself and your client up for success. Be inclusive of your own agenda, as well as the client's. Establish a mutually beneficial way forward. This meeting is one of many that when strung together form a *continuous engagement* that is the basis for an evolving and successful relationship.

Emotions and Disruptions

Although induction plays an important role in the often overlooked transitional moments of the day, it also plays a crucial role in the ability to navigate unanticipated complications. Induction reminds you that when things are difficult, you can do something about it. You don't have to be stuck in the problem with the accompanying emotions. You can move forward as you face these challenges.

When distractions arise: Focus your attention on the distraction and ask yourself: Is it useful and does it serve a purpose? Is there something compelling about this distraction? Does it offer some secondary gain? Can the distraction be beneficial in some way? If not, does it warrant turning away and recalibrating your efforts? If it happens in a meeting, how do you manage yourself and the meeting, return to the flow and the agenda? If it happens interpersonally, can you bring the dialogue back into focus? And if you are distracted, is there something you need that you are distracted *from*? Develop your method for managing distractions and work to maintain this method. If the source of the distraction is within you, it could be hunger, so remember to eat. If you are tired, develop your way of rest and recovery. If you are lonely, schedule social time and make it a priority.

When angry or upset: If you are angry, listen to this anger but be careful to only act on what it may be telling you once it has dissipated. Remember to detach the emotion from the object of the emotion. Anger is one emotion that can be potent enough to move us to unwise action and away from the process of building our relationships. Can you *turn your emotions to the wall?* Wait until the display of your emotion is dry, like a painting, before you show it to others.

Team Dynamics

While you practice the art of induction in your personal life, it can also apply to your team dynamics:

Take a moment, a pause, a breath, a moment of stillness, before beginning. Practice silence.

Be willing to risk simple expressions of kindness.

Acknowledge what is present in the room.

Remember to listen deeply. Be attentive, with all of your senses.

Allow yourself to live into the questions without prematurely seeking solutions or answers. Do this beyond your comfort zone and wait to speak until you can no longer contain yourself, and then wait a little longer.

Acknowledge the journey—what brought your team to this moment, what have you been through together, where are you heading, and how will you get there?

Show a form of gratefulness for the attendees. When it is true, gratitude has the potential to move people out of their expectations to observe and be fed information to a place where they resonate with the authentic message. If people feel valued, they will engage.

It is often helpful to have quick check-ins prior to starting the scheduled agenda.

Set the stage, arrange the tables, adjust the lights, start and end on time, check in with one another. By doing this you have established the *container*, a set of predictable norms for this and future meetings.

Be willing to be surprised and delighted by unexpected progress.

Acknowledge the context: the weather, venue, what is in the news that may concern people, the time of day, even the season.

Recognize who is in the room. Many cultures begin with acknowledging the elders as well as who, for whatever reason, cannot be with you that day.

Remember, clearly and cleanly closing out one phase of a meeting before transitioning to the next ensures the likelihood of the success of both.

Seal the success obtained, anchor the experience, and increase the half-life of the value achieved.

Induction's Kryptonite

Imagine what happens when the awareness of a child—or for that matter anyone of any age—is greeted with conflicting messages: a parent who promises one thing and does the opposite; a team leader who is duplicitous and communicates one thing but hides something else; or a colleague who makes an agreement and then *forgets* or denies that they created the expectation that they would follow through. In these cases, your awareness lands on a person, an object, or a situation and what becomes conscious is confusion. Awareness of something that is false causes confusion. This perceptual problem arises because you are aware of two messages, one that is communicated directly and one that is felt intuitively.

There are always forces that make accessing and wielding a power more difficult. Induction is no different. Its kryptonite comes in the form of inauthenticity, inflated ego, insecurity, and impatience. The following section explores these traps to help increase your awareness and identify the antidote.

Inauthenticity comes in many forms. When emotions are more performative than a true and authentic expression, other people will know what you are up to. These emotions are like empty calories; they fill you up, but they do not nourish. So what can you do about this? You can start by leaving a *pregnant pause*. Leave space and wait, breathe, and allow the deeper emotions to reveal themselves. Recognize when what you are doing is not working, and in that case, do anything else. Anything else is better than pursuing a failure that is revealing itself in the moment. As a friend of ours often says, "Just stop it, stop doing what doesn't work." Take the risk of trusting what you are actually thinking, feeling, and hoping for, and find a way to bring it into dialogue.

Inflated ego: Every human has an ego. That's not necessarily a bad thing; our egos are an essential part of healthy self-esteem and personal development. However, the line between self-assurance and self-centeredness can be difficult to navigate. Hubris can be alienating and unpleasant to be around. Learning to control the size of your ego is an integral part of the process of induction. Know when you are the right size for the situation.

Consider the possibility that, to the other person, you may not be all that interesting. Focus on others in the room and what is transpiring between you and them. Learn from the subtle dynamics that are present in every moment. If you shift your attention and involve others, the flow of the meeting will reestablish itself.

There is little advantage to holding on to resentment. When you begin to sour, you are increasingly moving into a world of your own making and intentionally disconnecting from your relationship, team, or even your career. Resentment is the one thing that can actually derail you from your goals. If you cannot move on from your resentments, it is time to ask for help. Ask a friend, a colleague, a coach, or even a therapist to walk through this hindrance with you. Do not remain isolated. Do not go it alone.

Having the wrong view is an overpowering assumption that you know what is best without tempering your position by recognizing that others will have contrasting experiences and views. Get feedback and regulate your words and behavior by asking and listening to the perspective of your team members, your peers, your allies. Remember, all things are impermanent. This too shall pass.

If you really need to justify yourself or your point of view, have at it. But remember that too much justification weakens your position. Standing on the ground of the Four Powers of Presence is a choice. Remember to take it. Move away from the feeling that you have to *prove yourself* and continue your determination to *be yourself.*

Insecurity may seem counterintuitive, but ego and insecurity are often two sides of the same coin. An individual's deep-rooted (and often unconscious) insecurities inform how they behave and present themselves to others.

There is wisdom in insecurity. It invites you to stop and self-examine. When you are feeling insecure, identify and allow those unwanted feelings. However, try not to get attached to them. It is only one perspective, in one moment, that has varying degrees of accuracy. You are getting acquainted with them, so that if they are active and function to distort your interactions with others, you can be aware of them and make decisions that work for you and not against you.

Insecurity can lead to a fear of being discovered. This is a tricky one. We all hide to varying degrees from time to time. One thing that we find helpful is to function with the understanding that all things are communicated. There is actually nowhere to hide. Practice forgiveness for yourself and for others.

When insecure, we begin to question our own legitimacy: the imposter syndrome. We all have this one as well. It connects to a fear of being discovered. Know that this is a state of mind. Fear comes and goes. When you perceive yourself through fear, you dull your clarity. You know that you are not seeing clearly, so loosen your identification with this tainted view. Also, trust that others, to some degree, recognize your value. That is why you are where you are. They cannot all be wrong.

Insecurity can make us want to please others to the extent

that it impedes our ability to act. Take a look at the definition of caretaking. From a psychological perspective, you seek to please others for one simple reason: you are not ready to feel what you would have to feel in order not to caretake. Examine in yourself what it would mean, what you would have to face, if you did not allow yourself to be motivated by having to please others. This is about you. It is not about them.

Doubting that the desired outcome can be reached is an indicator that you are becoming too inflated or grandiose. Seek clarity of reasonable goals but not at the expense of reaching beyond your perceived limitations. This is where *team* comes in. Don't go it alone. You need others who can see what you cannot and accept you for who you are.

Recognize and rest assured that others will judge you in both a positive and negative light. You cannot control this. However, you can remember that the judgment of others is just that—it is their judgment. It is most likely more about their projections and less about their ability to accurately perceive who you are. For the most part, judgment is not about the thing or person that is being judged. It is more about the person who is making the judgment.

Insecurity and its effects can make one feel uncomfortable. Our Western culture overly values comfort. Be willing to be disturbed and recognize that discomfort is necessary for growth, development, and managing your relationship with change.

Impatience is a common experience, especially in the workplace. We have all felt the frustration of having too much to do and not nearly enough time to do it. However, the urge to cut corners rarely pays off. These habits not only inhibit induction, but they create more problems along the way. Pay attention, and if you find yourself moving too quickly, breathe, pace yourself, and slow down. Leave a space between this moment and the next. Know when you or the team is distracted. Ask who in the room or meeting has what is necessary to bring everyone back on track. Impatience is not an efficient response to any situation. Increase your internal capacity by taking the time to think, feel, and act. Allow a more efficient tempo or cadence for what is happening around and within yourself. Calibrate yourself versus attempting to manipulate the external situation.

Overfatigue can exacerbate impatience. Get rest—by which we do not only mean sleep. Fatigue can send you plummeting into a downward spiral, where your ability to assess and accurately respond to the situations around you diminishes exponentially as you begin to burn out. There is a story of an executive who went to a therapist just for this reason: she was exhausted. The therapist quickly and accurately diagnosed her problem and suggested that she learn how not to burn the candle at both ends. The executive responded, "I already know that I am burning the candle at both ends, doctor. I am not here for your advice. I am here for more wax."

Prepare yourself ahead of time. Remember how debilitating it can feel to come into a situation unprepared. Focus on your method of organizing your day, your week, your career. Use your calendar as an integral component of your method.

Understand the underlying value of the check-in. This is a vital component of any meeting, whether with family, friends, or colleagues and clients. The check-in tells you where everyone in the room is coming from, where they are currently standing, and where they hope to go.

Before you speak or act . . . pause. Again, learn the value of the *pregnant pause.*

Wait and wonder long enough to explore the infinite possibilities and potential that is right in front of you. *Mind the gap.* In so doing, this will teach you to not fill the gap on impulse. Allowing yourself to settle into stillness, quietness, or silence takes practice. It is very difficult for most people. Practice letting go. Practice receiving. Practice being with what is. Practice silence.

Clarity arises when we face what makes us uncomfortable while, at the same time, we cultivate that which is seeking to unfold. Function with respect by living fully in each moment.

The Power of Induction is simple to understand and practice: whenever you transition from one moment to the next, shift your awareness from thinking about where you are leaving to where you are headed. Notice your thoughts, the feelings in your body, the emotional climate, the outer feel of the context you find yourself within. Additionally, remember that you are not alone in this context. Include all living things—the other people in the room, the unique relationship you have with each one of them, your conscious way of joining. Participate with intention, while allowing the rich infusion of information from each moment of perception. Engage fully in all transitions. Lead when called upon, and sit back and go for the ride when others know the direction.

Take this moment, relax, and close your eyes. Take three deep breaths. Open your eyes as you imagine, a soft image of entering a symphony hall prior to a performance. Notice the stage filled with musicians and their instruments. Some are just sitting down, while others are beginning to tune and play. As you take your seat, you feel the rough but comfortable material on the arm rests. You smell the scent of perfume. The lights have a slightly harsh glow, and you hear the cacophony of sound as instruments clamor into life. As more and more audience members arrive, you notice that they too are in different stages of preparation. Some taking jackets off, getting their seat just right, talking with the person next to them, texting, taking a breath, or just observing their surroundings. As the sound increases, you realize the musicians are attuning themselves as well as their instruments and, in turn, preparing the audience for the next moment—the performance. The uneven meandering mix of sounds fades out. Silence begins to embrace the hall. The lights dim. The air feels closer somehow. Suddenly, there is the resonant tap of the conductor's baton, the final transition. The performance begins. As this induction holds true, a sense of awareness is allowed to present itself. As the music reaches the audience, you are receptive as it affects your body, your mind, your spirit.

Your Induction Self-Assessment

Instructions: Use the scale below to assign a value to how each statement applies to you in your work setting. It is important to evaluate the statements honestly and without overthinking.

0 NEVER   **1** RARELY   **2** SOMETIMES   **3** USUALLY

_____ I imagine myself in the context of a meeting before I attend.

_____ I take time to center myself and recognize when I am leaving one activity to join another.

_____ When I present new information to a group or team, I assess the impact it could make before presenting it.

_____ By the time I sit down in front of my computer or enter my office or place of work, I have a clear idea of what I want to accomplish for the first thirty minutes of my day.

_____ When leading meetings, I ask for check-ins to see where each person stands prior to starting the scheduled agenda.

_____ I am comfortable with long pauses and stillness when working with others.

_____ I tend to focus on myself and what is of interest to me, while also recognizing the needs and interests of others.

SCORING: Add up the total number of points from each question.

Score less than 7: *You might have a long way to go before you reach induction, but the most important thing is to take stock of your strengths and weaknesses. This quiz can be the*

first step in achieving that awareness and initiating induction. Look through your answers and make a note of any questions that received a zero.

Score from 7 to 14: *You are finding a few times to access the power and have the opportunity to discover more. Be aware of your coming days and weeks and find one or two times that you may be able to consciously set an induction or two.*

Score from 15 to 20: *Inductions are integrated into your daily practice. Continue to use them where they make sense and are beneficial.*

Score of 21: *Nice work. Continue inviting consciousness of transitions into your daily life.*

To access free resources on cultivating the Power of Induction, please visit us at www.presentcompany .work or use this QR code.

The Power of
Awareness

Too Much Aim

The young man made a decision that would prove to be almost too difficult to bear. In a Buddhist monastery in the jungle just outside of Rangoon, he committed himself to meditation. For over three months, he practiced eighteen hours a day. Hour one: tracking his breath as it moved through his body as he sat—not the thought of the breath, or the image of the breath, but the pure sensation of it. Hour two: pacing the surface area of a small room—tracking the progression of each footfall as his foot lifted, moved through the air, and met the ground. For hour three, he sat again, and so it repeated, hour by hour, day by day, for 108 days. Perhaps you can imagine the strain this would put on a young man's mind. There was no reading, writing, talking, or eye contact allowed. There was no social interaction whatsoever, except during two meals each day, eaten in a small dining hall in complete silence.

For weeks, the experience was deeply rewarding. What a unique opportunity to learn a practice that dated back twenty-five hundred years. Hour by hour, his inner landscape opened. Thoughts, feelings, sensations, and images unfolded into the rich and diverse microclimate that is the human experience. The opportunity to sit and witness his mind, breath to breath, was extraordinary. Occasionally, a hill tribe, adorned with radiant colors of finely stitched natural fibers and expertly arranged hair, would sit just off the front porch of his small hut and watch him. Part of the practice was to have a weekly interview with a skilled master, who guided this rigor. Otherwise, he was alone.

What was the purpose of all this? To train his mind, strengthen his concentration, cultivate mindfulness, and build a psychological and physical resilience that few others are willing to practice.

But then, nine weeks in, with only a handful left, the pain began. Every breath, every thought, every movement was painful. The pain seemed to overwhelm his senses: at times it was physical—at others an emotional ache, the source undetectable. He didn't understand what could be causing this degree of discomfort. He counted down the moments until his weekly interview, desperately seeking the master's insight.

Finally, when the day arrived, the young man explained his dilemma to the translator, who then passed it on to the teacher. The master teacher listened, seemed to reflect for just a moment, and responded with three clear words: "Too much aim." The young man repeated the words back to himself in English. *Too much aim.* He waited for more.

Eventually, the master elaborated: "It is as though you are hungry and trying to spear a vegetable that sits on the plate in front of you. So you take your fork in hand, you pierce the vegetable, but then you persist, shattering the plate, driving the fork through the thick wooden table, and into the flesh of your knee. And you sit before me asking, 'Why am I in so much pain?' You are applying too much force with your mind. You need less effort, less certainty, less knowing. Practice being receptive and open to your experience. Receive what is right in front of you. Be more compassionate for yourself and your experience."

With the interview complete, the young man bowed and retreated. Within a few days, something in him had shifted. He was able to experience his thoughts as thoughts and not be so deeply absorbed. When he noticed an emotion or a feeling, it seemed to be the right size for the situation. Noticing hunger was just an experience of hunger, and it did not mean more than that. In a very real sense, he was able to find himself in every situation and no longer experienced the feeling of losing himself, his ground, his understanding of the situation. His pain subsided and the remainder of his stay in the monastery became different. Peace and equanimity began to greet him. He worked just as hard, practiced within the very rigorous schedule, and the practice became effortless.

Think of awareness as a flashlight. You can shine it anywhere you please. Direct it toward the landscape and take in the beauty of your surroundings: the scent of the air, the warmth of the sun or a cool breeze on your skin, the sounds in the distance. Shine awareness on the community of friends, family, acquaintances, and strangers that populate your world and the humanity that makes up your world reveals itself.

The light of awareness works inside as well. As you look upon your internal environment, you can register thoughts and the feelings in your body. You can shine your awareness into vague memories that come unannounced.

You can open your awareness as a loved one calls for your

attention. You can expand it to include an entire symphony of music. Or focus it so sharply, like a laser, on a task that requires specific and concentrated attention. With practice, your awareness can be calibrated to only include a specific depth of attention. When you do this, you are actually more conscious of, more receptive to, what lies in your peripheral awareness than you are of what is right before you.

See for yourself. Focus on something in the near distance. Soften your awareness without moving your eyes, and notice that your field of vision is now more inclusive of those things that are to your right and your left. Suddenly, you are using a wide-angle lens. Awareness is a dynamic power through which you are able to explore the world you inhabit to the degree and the depth of your choice.

Awareness is an extraordinary gift that you can take for granted. Awareness is so much a part of who you are that it is difficult to know for yourself how you experience it. As you are reading these words, look at the screen or the page of this book, pause for a moment, think about what you are doing. You can think about what occurred before you began reading. You can direct your awareness to what is happening around you. You can now direct your awareness to what is coming after you turn off your screen and put down this book. Awareness is a power that can be directed into the past by using your cognitive skills, into the present moment by using your senses, and into the future by using your imagination and vision. Wherever you place your awareness, you bring consciousness to the object of your awareness. You become conscious of the person across from you, the room you are in, the expectation of what will happen next, the memory of what happened last night. Awareness is a gift that allows you to be conscious of unlimited experience.

What you bring into your awareness generates consciousness of that thing. And this consciousness is internalized and informs you, for better or worse. Being able to choose what you bring into consciousness and what you leave unattended is an important ability. This discernment should tell you just how powerful your awareness can become. You can create a world that is vibrant and alive or one in which you perpetually encounter struggle. The determining factor is based on how you understand and train yourself to use the precious gift of your awareness.

This way of knowing is governed by the degree to which you are willing to be guided by what is being revealed. Choosing to receive what is uncovered, due to your awareness, allows you to be affected by what you see and feel. This is different from accepting only what you think you want to see and feel.

Aware That You Are Aware

The Power of Awareness can be investigated through a four-stage model: **unconscious incompetence**, **conscious incompetence**, **conscious competence**, and **unconscious competence**. This model was originally developed to assess the ability to teach, and we find it relevant to cultivating one's own awareness.[1] Together, these stages form a cycle that constantly informs us. As we experience our lives and the people around us, we find that it is necessary to manage each step in this process.

The foundational state, *unconscious incompetence*, hinges on the fact that most of us are unaware of our unawareness. You don't know that you don't know. Think again of the flashlight—no

---

1   Martin M. Broadwell, "Teaching for Learning (XVI.)," *The Gospel Guardian* 20, no. 41 (February 20, 1969): 1–3a.

matter where you point it, there will always be the periphery that is left unilluminated. If you remain unaware of the mystery and possibility of this uncharted territory, you inhibit an ability to truly understand your surroundings. Just like the glow of a flashlight, your field of awareness is limited, and much of the experience available gets lost in the shadows of your consciousness.

In this territory, just outside of conscious awareness, you lose an opportunity to explore yourself, others, and potential experience. It can happen on the first day of a new job: experience is filtered through familiar states of consciousness, inhibiting you from fully embracing the unknown. In the early stages of a new relationship, what is waiting to be discovered invites your awareness—about the other person and, equally important, about yourself with this person.

Although this stage of cultivated awareness holds the potential for failure, if you are open to the unknown presenting itself, it can also be rich with possibility. Not knowing that you don't know, as in unconscious competence, reminds us that we may never be aware of our failings until the results become problematic.

As you move through your day, it is all too easy to get stuck in this state of unconscious incompetence. Like a spotlight that refuses to move, not knowing can become an isolating constraint around your experience. Even as you transition from place to place, from moment to moment, the perimeter of your attention remains fixed, effectively excluding new input and insight from your experiences. In a new job, unfamiliar location, or new relationship, there is so much that falls outside the frame of your awareness. You only know what you know, and because the majority of these new experiences are driven by the unknown, you end up having a limited capacity to direct your awareness.

When everything is unfamiliar, it is impossible to take stock of all the novelty and uncertainty that you encounter. Life lives on around you, while you track the narrow confines of the familiar.

A very direct way to remedy the narrowing of your experience is to approach each moment with curiosity, while accepting the discomfort of the unknown. In these moments, be willing to be disturbed, excited, expectant. Live into your anticipation and suspend the need to understand, make sense, and interpret. Seeking comfort in answers or certainty is like building a fence around the field of your consciousness—it prematurely and unnecessarily limits your ability to open your awareness.

Let curiosity guide you. In any given situation, ask yourself the question "What do I not know that I don't know?" This will fuel the transition to the next stage of awareness—*conscious incompetence*, or knowing that you don't know. This transition often requires revelations, the kind that you have probably experienced multiple times. Think of the times when you found that you were using a word in the wrong context, singing a song lyric incorrectly, using an appliance the wrong way, or taking a roundabout way to your favorite restaurant only to discover that it is accessible through a shorter, more direct route.

These moments of revelation happen when you turn around after going in the wrong direction and recognize that the place you are looking for is actually behind you. Once you realize that you have been unaware of your own unawareness, the reality of the moment thrusts itself into consciousness. This realization can be met with either complacency or curiosity. The complacent response leaves you stuck at this stage. To be conscious of your incompetence, you must do something about it. Regulating the depth and the breadth of your awareness is that mechanism that will give you this choice.

For example, imagine you learned that there is no hand gesture that means the same thing in all cultures or countries. For example, thumbs up in one country can mean *good job* or *it's all okay*, whereas in another country or culture it can mean *up yours* or *go to hell*. What you do with this revelation is your choice. For some, it may be *So what, I am going to keep gesturing the way I gesture, and if others get offended or misinterpret what I am saying, they can deal with it*. For others, this new awareness would push them into action. They might take it upon themselves to explore a range of common gestures and determine how they differ culturally.

How you respond to this state of conscious incompetence is a good indicator of whether you have a fixed mindset or a growth mindset. Those with a fixed mindset might be aware of an area of ignorance or uncertainty, and they might even know how to assuage it, but they are not yet motivated to *act* on it. By contrast, those with more of a growth mindset see this revelation as an invitation. Knowing that you don't know is fundamental to cultivating the Power of Awareness. It is the central practice that influences every incremental step involved in learning, growth, and positive change. This choice unveils the richness and endless possibilities that can be found in your experience.

The next step in this cycle, **conscious competence**, can be both painful and euphoric, uncomfortable and satisfying, terrifying and invigorating. Doing the work in this stage forces you to look into yourself and face certain truths you may wish to ignore or deny. Choosing the path of curiosity leads to the desire to understand what may have just been revealed. This stage is one that seeks depth and breeds further awareness and continued learning.

In a practical sense, imagine that you have just learned, through a 360-degree survey from your coworkers, that they perceive your communication style as aggressive. This comes as a complete surprise. Your intention has never been to be aggressive, yet this is what people are saying. You have been thrust into knowing that you didn't know and are faced with a choice. Ignore what they say and keep doing what you do? Apologize for the way that you have been communicating, but don't change anything moving forward? Ask for further feedback on how you could be perceived as less aggressive in your communications, then begin to put what you learned into practice? Explore if others in your life feel similarly? Look to past relationships and seek those peoples' thoughts as well? Seek out the root of your aggressive behavior and begin to address it? Practice a higher level of awareness in all of your future communications?

In much of our work with executive teams, we offer a mirror, so each individual can receive critical feedback as both a leader and a team member. In one case, the CFO of a large nonprofit would consistently disrupt meetings. He recognized his tendency to get angry and yell, which he realized was a result of not having enough time to process his feelings. When he gave himself just a little time to sit with his emotions and digest his frustration, he was able to reengage at the right level to achieve the intended results. Once this behavior was brought to light, he was able to self-regulate and clean up the discord. In another case, through mirroring and high-quality feedback, we helped the new CEO of a financial firm see that his need to establish likeability undercut his authority when it was time to make decisions. Highly interactive feedback invites a leader *to know what they didn't know* and puts them on the precipice of trying to better understand the unknown. This takes commitment, grit, patience, compassion, and a lot of vulnerability.

Many choose not to take it on fully. Those who do take it on begin to see what working as a team member really means and what can be achieved by taking this risk. Competency, in this example, is exhibited by a determination to consciously make the change.

The fourth stage, *unconscious competence*, requires a level of mastery that is difficult to attain—and often even harder to maintain. Once you reach a certain threshold of skill and understanding, many tasks, processes, and practices can become automatic—that is, they are performed with little conscious thought or effort. For most, physiological processes for functioning normally or daily routines such as brushing their teeth or driving to work easily become habitual. For some, even the most specialized skill, such as playing a musical instrument or intricate surgery, can become an intuitive process.

This stage of awareness, often seen as most desirable by leaders and their team members, can be a double-edged sword. If left unchecked, not knowing that you know can start to look more like overconfidence. Habitual processes can lead to a diminishing feedback loop, allowing you to detach from the impact of your behavior. Perhaps you had to complete a task that you've done countless times at a high level. You don't think too much about it, and the quality begins to slip. The unconscious aspect of this stage can sometimes result in a lack of presence, which in turn can affect one's competence.

To avoid these pitfalls, you can purposefully take yourself back to the first stage by asking, *What is it that I may be missing in performing this task, addressing this situation, or assessing my impact on this relationship?* We look at these stages as a cycle, and those seeking awareness are faced with the opportunity to consistently and proactively move through these four stages.

Self-Awareness

A prideful young man armed with a PhD, a few years of training and experience in his field, and a bucketload of other credentials went to a wise man with one question: "What can I do to save the world?" The wise man assessed the young man for a moment and replied, "I don't think the question is 'What can I do to save the world?' Rather, you might consider asking, 'What can I do to save the world from myself?'"

Knowing yourself is the greatest gift you can give yourself, your loved ones, and humankind. This has been true for millennia in various cultures and languages—from prophets and gurus, through rulers and teachers, to bloggers and tweeters. What follows is a simple and practical method that will allow you to recognize, access, and utilize the different states of self-awareness in daily life.

State of Self

Before you can effectively take stock of your surroundings, it is important to look inward and track your own intentions.

The body: The experience of the body is a vast area of discovery: breath, movement, pleasant feelings, discomfort, itching, aches, pains, and more. As you investigate, right now while you are reading, notice that your experience of the body is in a constant state of flux. What draws your attention in this moment may not exist in the next. What do you focus on? What do you notice?

Thoughts: We are thinking all of the time. Notice your thoughts as you read these words. Do you hear the words in your mind? Do you experience them in the foreground or the background?

How are your thoughts interacting with the words and ideas on these pages? Do you ignore the thoughts, do you direct them, or do you merely watch your thoughts as they float by like clouds in the sky?

Choices: Once you are aware of your body, thoughts, and feelings, you can cultivate the ability to direct your focus. This shifting of focus is what many call mindfulness. *Mindfulness* is the ability to open your consciousness to what is seeking your awareness and choosing to stay present.

Making decisions is one way to filter your experience. Every choice *for* something is also a decision *against* something else. As you move toward *this* with your awareness, you move away from *that*. But it is not as simple as deciding what to order from a restaurant menu or selecting a new movie to watch. Attention is often conditioned so heavily that it can feel as though you're reacting to certain stimuli in your environment. The shiny object, the unwanted feeling in your belly, the thought of something you are not ready to face, the imagined criticism of a colleague or rumination on a past mistake—without your conscious choice, any one of these can determine the course of your attention. You can actually cultivate and limit your capacity to pay attention, as your attention moves away from the unexpected and back to the familiar, basically through habit. However, when your awareness is more discerning and open to a greater flow of experience, the possibilities are endless. You can direct your awareness in ways to consciously determine what you hear, see, smell, and feel. It is often said that through negotiation of the obstacles, you find your way.

State of Other

With a deeper sense and awareness of self, you are able to see others from a more solid and balanced foundation.

Michael tells the following story:

> Walking down the city street, I encountered a young person sitting cross-legged on the sidewalk holding up a sign. He was smiling slightly and waving calmly as people passed. I caught myself about to ignore him, as I made the assumption that he was seeking money. Then I stopped and read the sign: testing human kindness. I made direct eye contact and waved back and then proceeded to witness a good fifty people walk by without acknowledging the sign or the person sitting behind it.

What are you willing or able to allow into your consciousness? Do you sort for the pleasant and comfortable, or are you willing to open up to the unfamiliar, disturbing, or even the unpleasant? *I am happy to focus on this but not on that. I can listen to you later, but not now. I can accept that you will not be able to meet this expectation but must insist that you meet that one.* At all times, you will find yourself accepting many things into your consciousness but also rejecting just as many. Your attention is yours to use. How will you choose what you do with it? What could you learn from what you choose to ignore?

Often, there is quite a bit to learn from the unwanted or unknown. Taking stock of what you tend to overlook can be revealing.

Tim tells the following story:

During a morning walk, my wife and I heard someone call out, "Hello, Tim." Ahead of us, we saw a friend of ours meandering down the beach toward us. His gait was random, and we wondered if he was nursing a hangover from the night before. We paused and chatted with him for a while. Well, his *wobbly way* took on a whole new meaning. He had just sailed into the harbor in a small boat, having completed a very long journey from Hawaii, nearly four thousand miles away. He still had his *sea legs*, adapted to moving about on a pitching and rocking sea and not the static nature of the sandy beach.

Some days, awareness just doesn't seem to help, and the mind can be too quick to judge. When you know that, for a variety of reasons, you are filtering your experience to include the familiar and exclude the unwanted or unfamiliar, you might say that you are consciously biased. The ability to recognize your biases or the biases of another person opens up the possibility of true change.

Framing your participation with another person or your surroundings through the lens of a witness allows you to participate without becoming identified. Observation doesn't mean that you are necessarily detached and unaffected. It does mean, however, that you are not absorbing your experience into your limited world of ideas and values. You are informed without preference and not just seeing what you want to see. The normal filters you use to navigate the world do not function as they usually do. You may take in more than you are used to, see more than you normally see, feel more than usual, and, as a net result, begin to shift how you think about your experience.

Witnessing is a level of consciousness in which you are aware of the sensory data that you are gathering while, at the same time, being aware of the experience of gathering that information. You are aware that you are aware.

State of Relationship

Relational awareness is distinctly different from awareness of ourselves or awareness of another. There is a third thing, the relationship, that is real and yet slightly intangible. As Tim's therapist used to say to him, "There is you, there is your partner, and then the third thing is the relationship." It is very difficult to quantify a relationship. You know they exist, but because they don't have a voice, they can be difficult to hear. Because they don't have a body, they are elusive and challenging to see.

So how do you attune yourself to the relationship? Is it based on how you think about yourself and what you want or give? Is it based on the person or people you are involved with and how they think and feel: partner, team members, family members, friends? As you focus on yourself and the degree to which you are able to perceive those in your life, focus on your six senses. As you look at someone, be aware that you see them, feel what they might be feeling, investigate what they may be thinking. You have heard the expression "Walk a mile in my shoes." Well, yes, consider doing this. Tune into the people you are with and imagine what it must be like for them right in this moment.

Questions to Consider

Do you know how your relationship is experienced by the person you are with? Imagine what a witness would experience, if they followed you throughout the day and observed you with this other person.

Can you gain an accurate sense of how the other person experiences you? Do they enjoy themselves; are they challenged, inspired, motivated?

What do they do with you in their experience? Can you tell what they are thinking and feeling as a result of being with you? Can you imagine yourself as experienced through their eyes, their thinking, and their feelings, and look back at yourself?

Do you recognize them without preconceived notions and simply through how in this moment they are choosing to reveal themselves to you? Ask yourself:

As I listen to you, experience you, even love you, do I do so in my world, your world, or our joint world in common?

At any given moment, can I tell the difference between projecting my feelings, thoughts, and opinions onto you? Do I accurately perceive your thoughts, feelings, and opinions as separate from my own?

ACTIONS THAT SERVE UNAWARENESS:

Living in your own reality: The assumption that you live in a separate reality that is not fully interdependent is our definition of arrogance.

Acting as if: When you are not aware of others, you wander in the relational context as a caricature of yourself. You act *as if*, as opposed to acting *in relationship to*. *As if* is a generated reality based on your individual thoughts and feelings. *Acting in relationship to* is a lived experience rooted in the present moment, experienced by many on multiple levels of consciousness. You build your connections as you would build a house of solid timber.

Nothing is ever enough: The chair could be more comfortable, the room cooler, the weather more pleasant. When you shift your attention solely to your own experience of something, you no longer experience yourself in the context where your body resides. Rather, you become identified with a self-referential interpretation of the moment, which is not the actual moment and which is not necessarily inclusive of others.

Denial of your own experience: If you are like many people, you seek personal change, begin to grow in the direction you hoped to develop, and then for some reason choose not to risk continuing because—*It is too hard, I can't afford the time, it is not important anyway.*

Denial of the feedback from others: You ask for feedback, and people give it to you. You say thank you and then, as time passes, you do nothing about it. Or, in the moment, you defend or justify the very behavior that is being highlighted for a necessary change. By disallowing feedback, you actually shut down your capacity to internalize what others are telling you, resulting in a diminished capacity to remain open and aware.

Avoidance of feeling: You consciously avoid the conversations that need to be had because you don't want to feel what you would have to feel in order to have the conversation—take the risk of hearing what you don't want to hear or say what you are not prepared to say.

The lone cowboy syndrome: You feel like you are the only one who knows what to do, so you go it alone. When you are out riding the range, making your own decisions, you don't have to deal with the others back at the ranch.

The cobbler's culture: There is an old adage, *A cobbler's children have no shoes*. In companies and teams, it shows up again and again. What you espouse to practice at a high level with your customers, you neglect to practice with your team. The core values that are socialized throughout the company are not being embodied and lived by the leaders who came up with those values in the first place. This is the person who claims to stand for honesty, yet lies; the team that puts accountability first, yet never takes ownership when things go wrong; the company that champions diversity, yet engages in misogynistic, racist, or homophobic behavior.

ACTIONS THAT SERVE UNAWARENESS:

During a meeting with your team: Take a moment to check your body language, the tone and tempo of your voice, then check your breath. What messages do you hope to be sending to others?

During a one-on-one: Focus on what is being said versus what you want to say.

Upon returning home from work: Recognize the reactions you get from others as you make your presence known.

Upon entering the office or place of work: Note how you walk through the space. How do others engage you, or do you engage them first? Make a conscious choice to reach out and connect.

During a meeting with a customer: Make them the sole focus of your awareness.

When distractions arise: Recognize them for what they are. Determine their value, if any. This is a first step in lessening them as a distraction.

Recognize your right to be here: We all do have a place here, in this moment, in this context, on this Earth because of all that has led us to this moment. There is no need to assert it, just live within it.

Acknowledge the other's right to be here: I may disagree with you. You might push my buttons. You may annoy me. I may not understand what you stand for. But your right to be here is not in question.

The True You

Questioning is a great first step in developing awareness. Knowing that you don't know is a start and can be applied to people, places, things, tasks, and experiences. Taking a deeper look at yourself is a next step to exploring what you feel in a given moment or how others may perceive you. Once the questions are discovered, they may lead you to the answers and to a transition into new possibilities.

The moment is primed through an induction, which allows the mind to be awakened and aware. Now it is safe enough to be your genuine self, inclusive of the other.

Your Awareness Self-Assessment

Instructions: Use the scale below to indicate how each statement applies to you in your work setting. It is important to evaluate the statements honestly and without overthinking your answers.

0 NEVER   **1** RARELY   **2** SOMETIMES   **3** USUALLY

_____ When interacting with others, I focus on what I want or need to say versus what is being said.

_____ At my place of work, I don't recognize the reactions that I get from others.

_____ When distractions arise, I don't recognize them for what they are.

_____ I am consciously avoiding conversations that need to be had with others.

_____ I don't practice what I preach.

_____ I make observations of others that are actually judgments.

_____ I choose to remain consciously incompetent.

SCORING: Add up the total number of points from each question.

Score of 21: *What a perfect opportunity to begin to practice a deeper level of self-awareness. If you find yourself rejecting this statement, that is the best place to start.*

Score from 15 to 20: *You might have more work to do to employ the Power of Awareness more consistently, but the most important thing is to take stock of your strengths and*

weaknesses. This quiz can be the first step in achieving that deeper level of awareness. Look through your answers and make a note of any questions that received a 3.

Score from 8 to 14: *You are finding several opportunities to access the power and have the opportunity to discover more. Look through your coming days and weeks and determine one or two times when you may be able to set an intention to be more aware in specific situations.*

Score from 2 to 7: *Awareness is enmeshed in your daily practice. Continue to recognize the benefits of using awareness where and when it makes sense for you, others, and your relationships.*

Score of 0 or 1: *We could share some thoughts here, but you're already aware.*

To access free resources on cultivating the Power of Awareness, please visit us at www.presentcompany .work or use this QR code.

The Power of
Authenticity

Alex, the CEO of a leading technology start-up, earned a PhD from a top-tier school. She worked her way through the ranks, honing her interpersonal skills along the way. She had a good sense of humor, an affable disposition, and a wonderful smile. She listened well and said the right thing at the right time. She was able to connect with almost anyone in any situation and was liked by everyone. But as the organization began to scale up, Alex's leadership became patterned and repetitive. Her effectiveness stalled, and she seemed to have become a caricature of herself. People on her team began to say things behind her back. *Something has changed. She seems like a different person. It's like she is disconnected from what is really going on. Trust in us seems to have . . . I don't know . . . been lost.*

Alex needed to make a transition. The source from which she drew her energy, power, and authority had shifted. In the early stages of her team's development, Alex knew exactly where and how to connect to achieve results. However, the organization's rapid growth shifted Alex's points of contact with others. As priorities changed, she was no longer consistently connecting with the team, if at all. As a result, Alex's engagements were less authentic and even forgotten. Her interactions became more *efficient* and transactional. She devolved into thinking, "It takes too much time," "It slows the process," "I have more important things to attend to." As Alex's focus shifted to getting things done, her attention to process and how the outcomes were achieved receded. It became easier to stop seeing the team as human potential but instead as assets to be leveraged, drive results, and meet the bottom line. Coaching turned into blaming. Frustration devolved the culture and anger became normalized. She was not making the necessary modifications to remain effective as an authentic leader, and she needed help.

Many of the large, well-known company leadership programs tend to include a section something like *Authentic Leadership*, *Authentic Self-Branding*, or *Being True to You*. These concepts are challenging for program participants. To begin with, it is necessary to define authenticity, and this is difficult.

Think about yourself for a moment. How do you define authenticity? What does it mean for you to be authentic? Consider these observations by other leaders who have reflected on this question:

» *I am authentic when I reference someone, a team member, in a discussion with another team member in such a way that I would be comfortable with them being in the room and overhearing my discussion.*
» *Authenticity comes from my heart, when my words and my behaviors are consistent with how I feel.*

» *Even when I am afraid of what may lie ahead, after careful consideration and reflection, I take the actions necessary to do the right thing.*
» *I try to have all of my actions and decisions tempered by my focus on long-term results for the organization and short-term decency in all of my interactions.*

Authenticity is not about your preferences and what you think is right or wrong. Your authenticity is not revealed in how you hope to be. Nor is it an expression of how you think you should be. And it is certainly not as you imagine yourself to be perceived by others. Authenticity is about *one thing* and *one thing only*.

Authenticity is found in your capacity to be just as you are, warts and all, and to manage the tension of this realization. It reveals itself in your communication style. This capacity allows you to hold in consciousness two dynamic factors, so that one isn't potent enough to defeat the other.

» *I am late and feel bad, and I need to accept how others feel about it.*
» *I do have warts, they are visible, and I am not going to hide them or be defensive when others notice.*
» *I am smart, I am educated, and I am responsible for leading, but in this moment, I am not confident.*

This list could go on forever. We all face these internal conflicts on a daily basis. However, authenticity is a capacity that allows you to accept yourself, just as you perceive yourself in these moments. A few authentic self-reflections:

» I stay in the conversation, though I am uncomfortable.
» I remind myself to listen and feel, which is not easy for someone who wants to find a solution for a problem right now.

» It is important for me to keep all of my agreements. I know what it is like to be disappointed.

What does it mean to be authentic from the perspective of the people who you are with? How does your authenticity reveal itself as you imagine or perceive how others look at you? Can you hold your happiness and still feel and think about how another person may be struggling? Can you accept your gifts or talents without becoming overly identified with them? Can you know that you don't know, yet still stay in a field of inquiry with your colleagues? Can you allow yourself to feel insecure, yet still perform as the professional you are? This list is also endless. Take a moment to generate your own, by asking, *In this moment, what personal conflicts am I aware of?* Can you embrace these conflicts without having to act as if they do not exist? Can you find a way to manage how you feel without becoming *one-sided* and succumbing to the trap of right versus wrong, good versus bad?

There are *near enemies* of authenticity—statements or postures that look like you are being yourself but are in fact an expression of something else. Your self-expression of *me being me* can easily be interpreted by others as *being all about you,* especially when it comes to how you communicate, how you deliver feedback, and how you greet people or the fact that you don't. What you define as *being authentic* can be couched in *what worked for you in the past.* Authenticity does not exist outside of inner conflict. Your authenticity must include how it affects those around you. Authenticity is not one-sided, and it is usually relationally dependent. You do not need to explain that you are being authentic, but you do have to acknowledge how your behavior affects others. What is your authentic self?

These inner conflicts arise in moments when your inner clarity is clouded. Your perceptions of yourself or others has become colored by your mood, your ability to pay attention or remain present. Your capacity to discern your thoughts and feelings from those around you can be messy. When this occurs, peel the onion to the next layer. Find out what is influencing your ability to clearly see what is influencing your perceptions.

» Know that what you perceive is filtered by your mood and the condition of your mind in any given moment. In recovery programs, we often use the acronym HALT. *Stop* and pay attention if you are *hungry, angry, lonely,* or *tired.* Any one of these conditions can affect how you perceive a situation and influence your perceptions, thinking, and behavior.

» Know that engaging with what is seeking your attention is only limited by your capacity to receive it. You have five senses that are constantly presenting the opportunity to expand your consciousness. Just now, pause and shift your attention to hearing. Notice your increased capacity to listen both to what is around you and what is inside of you. Pause, and shift your awareness to your body. Breathe. Notice the complexity of stimuli available to your awareness. Take this moment to explore the sensations or feelings in your body and notice your increased awareness compared with that of a few moments ago. Allow this awareness to expand and open your body and mind.

» Due to your intention and ability to direct your awareness internally or externally, you can reveal yourself to yourself. How you use your awareness determines your experience, by what you focus your attention on. If you have a concern about how you are being perceived by others, get the information directly from them, either by asking or by your own ability to *read* how they experience you. Your thoughts about how you are being perceived are just that: thoughts.

» Know that what is true in your experience of yourself, in this moment, will change. Maybe it just did.

Authenticity is a fluid experience. It is difficult to know who you are until you arrive. Your chances of connecting and being perceived as authentic increases if you first reveal what is hidden behind the curtain. Imagine the following scenarios. How would you feel about the participant's ability or willingness to relate authentically?

» Your team leader discloses that she grew up in a family culture where no one ever said what they were really thinking or feeling. The communication in her family was passive-aggressive and caused her a great deal of stress, anxiety, and emotional trauma. She tells you that she thinks this is why she has become very direct and to the point, for fear of recreating or furthering more passive-aggressive communications. She acknowledges that her style of communication may be off-putting and that she is working on it. If she admits this to herself and reveals it to you, she feels she is being authentic.

» He is late to a meeting and instead of using traffic as an excuse, he states that he should have considered leaving earlier and his intention was not to be late or show any sign of disrespect. Is he taking ownership for his actions and being authentic?

Disclosure of *where you are coming from*, as a statement about yourself, can put others at ease. It opens the communication to the other side of the equation and includes the listener in anything that may influence their ability to stay connected.

However, would this degree of disclosure put you in a position of giving or receiving too much information? Would it then require you to open and risk the exposure of your authentic self? Would you be able to manage your discomfort in such a way as to remain open and receptive? Does this make you an authentic listener?

Collusions in the Inauthentic

» The leader who says that something is true when they know it is not. And you know it is not true when you hear them say it.

» Agreements made that neither one of you intend to keep.

» The colleague who says that they will do something, and, given past experience, both of you know it will not happen, but you do not say anything.

» The friend that says they will meet you at a function, when they have no intention of attending. And you actually know this at the time.

» The peer who does not offer a counter opinion, when it is evident they disagree.

» The manager that never reveals their mistakes. Everyone else knows it, but they are never or seldom called on it.

» The partner that does not share their true feelings and sabotages the depth to which the partnership functions. And you go along with it.

» When *that is how I feel* does not translate as authentic. It is a communication serving some other purpose.

» The parent that persistently tries to smooth over their feelings and the feelings of their children and no one says anything.

These acts, though they may be well intentioned, are insincere. They create a double message. You end up intuitively internalizing one message, while you are being told something else.

In his book *Falling Awake*,[2] Mark Burger tells us that during a visit to the Cincinnati Art Museum, he overheard a lecture on Roman sculpture. The teacher explained to her class that the flaws of a sculpture where often hidden by an application of wax. When the cracks were not hidden, the piece was considered sincere, without wax. When we leave the wax off, we reveal our vulnerability. The path to our true self begins to open, allowing others to peer into our authenticity. Without acknowledging our flaws, and our inclination to hide them, authenticity is not possible. A false communication designed to hide how we are thinking, feeling, or behaving creates a false, provisional self. It is not the same as the self that emerges when we accept, at a deeper level, that which we cannot control and decide not to hide. We may decide to hold private our thoughts and feelings, which is often the right way to go. However, when we construct a false self and hide behind it, we are taking steps away from choosing authenticity.

Perfect Flaws: Like Me, Follow Me, Want to Be Me!

Much has been written about our Facebook, Twitter, and Instagram selves. These online, perfected images are distancing all of us from our true humanity. We are all subjected to this possibility: Your curated existence in photos, tweets, and posts show your happy life, perfectly posed and filled with rainbows and butterflies. Your flaws are airbrushed away. The world sees

---

2   Mark Burger, *Falling Awake* (self-pub., Lulu Publishing Services, 2015).

what you want them to see. The smiles, the cool locations, the amazing times you are having. The time it takes to get the pic just right, post it, and wait for the response of your "friends" takes you away from being present for yourself. This moves you into a fabricated reality—and, perhaps without knowing it, you bury your true experiences, feelings, and thoughts. And most tragically, you are left alone in that experience.

This *as-if*, the self-generated persona, takes you into a competitive mode of who can cover up their flaws quicker and more consistently. If you see a friend, colleague, or celebrity posting a snippet of the good life, you may feel *less-than*, so you "like" the post, even though you are actually envious. You may then craft another perfectly flawless post that will cause others who see it to want to do the same. The cycle is self-perpetuating. We act as if we are coming closer together in our identification with one another's experience, when in fact we are cycling further and further apart.

Ironically, the message that is being promoted and projected on screens and psyches is one of perfection: perfect relationships, perfect smiles, perfect framing, perfect clothing, perfect bodies, perfect weather, perfect flaws. This translates into having no flaws, because *flaws* just aren't worth following, won't get you *likes*, and just aren't cool.

This ended up being the case for Alex, the CEO we talked about earlier. She was caught up in covering her self-perceived flaws. The other executives felt that Alex didn't trust them anymore. They stopped sharing what was really happening and felt isolated and disconnected. What they did share was also false. This impacted their performance and engagement and even caused a few members to consider leaving the organization. There is an interesting question to be asked in this scenario:

"Did Alex abandon the team, or did the team abandon her?" By not telling the truth about their experience, how much were each of them participating in the team's breakdown?

There is something that can be done about this estrangement and self-imposed exile. With help, Alex and her team began a process of alignment by focusing on and instituting procedural structure based on the following understandings:

» When people on the team feel safe, you can talk about anything.
» Mutual respect and purpose are prerequisites for safety.
» Communication is the result, not the intention.

The next step for Alex was to understand that her behavior was the reason the team was not feeling safe, respected, or aligned around a common purpose. To reveal what was hiding under the wax, Alex began to inquire into the following:

1. *What am I holding on to?*
2. *What would it take to engage with the team in a positive cohesive manner?*

Alex sat with each of these questions for some time and finally came back with the following:

1. What am I holding on to? *Ownership. I am scared to let go of things that may actually fall under the responsibilities of others. It's not that I don't think they can do it, but I feel like, as a CEO, it's all on me if it doesn't work out, so I don't want to let it go.*
2. What would it take for me to engage with the team in a positive, cohesive manner? *Surrendering ownership. Explaining why I have done what I have done. Listening. Being more aware*

that I often move on to decision mode, when team members may want or need to engage in more discussion.

We facilitated a process of meetings that included helping the team set the stage for true presence through short inductions. Once settled, we gave them a prompt to think about what they were willing to risk today and what they would like to accomplish regarding their individual performance. This primed the team to risk authenticity, which Alex provided, unprompted.

Alex began the process by sharing: *I am scared. I have never done this before. This is my first time being a CEO. I'm feeling the pressure to deliver, and I don't know if we can. If I can.* The response, after several seconds of silence, was impactful. One member of the team revealed, quite passionately, that he and the rest of the team had Alex's back, no matter what. *This is our first time too. Just include us, and we are here for you. We're all in this together.*

When you act *as if* you are connected, as though you see yourself mirrored by the other, when in fact the other does not experience a similar connection, you are entangling that person in a false narrative. Relationship, authentic engagement, is largely based on the reactions of others. Entangling others in your self-generated behavior enlists them in your performance, through your words, behaviors, and even your thoughts. Acting as if you are in the moment is confusing and disorienting.

When you perform, you are presenting two sets of information. One set is telling others that you are here and present. The other set is their actual experience, which would be incongruent with the first. This false position communicates conflict. An authentic position communicates resolution. The false separates; the authentic invites connection.

To move from the enmeshment that results from a false

engagement requires a level of determination and practice. You have to practice coming back to one set of information: the experience of your own thoughts, feelings, perceptions, and behaviors while also registering the thoughts, feelings, perceptions, and behaviors of the other. This is a moment of empathic accord, two separate instruments in need of being tuned to the same key and scale.

By manufacturing *who* you are, you are basing your behavior on how you imagine a person perceives you. Unfortunately, when you meet that same person in the future, you may have to reconstruct yourself from the memory of that previous, shared experience. This is often difficult to replicate, requiring you to continually look back to reconstruct who you were then at the expense of who you are today.

When you act *as if*, you invest into an incremental flow of deception. We all have a potential to do this over and over again. You act as if you understand or have the skills necessary for the task. As you *practice* your unique way of being, you can cultivate a critical mass of intention, which then becomes a context with the potential to restrict and even deaden your growth and development. Forgetting who you really are, you are lost to a world of your own making.

How do you unravel this conundrum? You need to find the resources to reset, so that you become conscious of how incompetent you have become. You don't need to fix who you are: you have to remember who you were. You need to turn inward and greet those forgotten parts left behind. In doing so, you will most likely encounter discomfort. If you cannot allow yourself to feel this discomfort, you risk moving away from who you are, creating an inner tension that will place unforeseen limits on you and encourage the return to your false way of being.

Amir, a forty-year-old, high-functioning CEO of a booming start-up, lived a life where every challenge was met with enthusiasm. Seemingly, he had no limits. He could work late into the evening, returning home for a cold dinner and conversation with his wife before kissing his sleeping children. And then rise at five a.m. for a run. According to him, his wife and his executive team adapted and embraced his drive. However, after conducting interviews, he found that many on his team felt as though they were working alongside a robot. His high efficiency hindered most of the team members. Amir could not accept limitations in himself and, consequently, could not accept limitations in others. Challenges and problems lingered too long on the drawing board because decisions—important ones—were not being made. Amir was patterning himself to not register natural limitations of time and energy.

You have to turn outward and consciously pay close attention to how you are being perceived. This takes courage. Your true self or true persona opens you up to true engagement. The thoughts about yourself disrupt your actual relationship with yourself. The self is not something to be known; it is something that is revealed over time.

The self is better at hiding than you will ever be at finding it. When you are present, you don't seek to find the self. Much like spending time with a tree, a child, your partner—you are here and engaged, soon to let go. And if fully present, this cycle of engagement and letting go repeats at an extraordinary rate. Imagine that as you watch a movie, the old-time projector is slowed so each frame proceeds across the scene one at a time. To know your true self, you settle in moment to moment and receive the experience, one frame at a time. This understanding of yourself is revealed through the eyes and hearts of those around you.

The Beauty of Imperfection

Wabi-sabi, a traditional Japanese concept, reminds us that it is possible to accept imperfections in life, art, and form—and even to find appeal in flaws and impermanence. There is a beauty to your imperfections. Transience reminds you that each moment refreshes the imprint of the previous moment. Moments arrive with their stamp of originality. Your communication and connections can be a beauty of imperfection—unique in their authentic creation.

Authenticity carries a historic sense of *authority*. Being authentic does not mean that you should not fear what people think of you. It does not mean that you have to figure out how to be in closer proximity to who you think you are. It *does* mean, however, that you have to stand on your own authority. It does not mean that there is a better, truer you that—if only you could quell the internal dialogue—could express itself *authentically*. To be *authentic* means to be true to each moment and hold that moment with as much consciousness as possible.

Alchemy of the Authentic

How you hold the conversation determines what is communicated. When your thoughts, words, and behaviors are authentic, you are consistent with how you see or experience yourself, including your flaws. As the author of your experience, you are primed to emerge in the relational context or social system as authentically present. Through an expression of your authenticity, an alchemy arises molding and informing your experience as it shapes and casts your interactions. This relational environment that arises out of authentic presence creates a context that invites the following:

» Clarity of intention, consciousness, and mindful functioning
» Realignment from an individual perspective to a group perspective
» Cultivation of an ecosystem, milieu, or culture in which unconscious influences are revealed and accepted
» Revelation of mental models and the thought processes that reside behind the decisions we make
» Openness to exploring a variety of mental models that can better serve you
» Highlighting obstacles that you knowingly and unknowingly place in your way, and their effect on outcome and sustainability
» Recognition of the wake you make, revealing the impact you wish to have as you use and reshape your conversations

When we exercise the power of authenticity, we hold the potential for true presence to arise, ensuring alignment between what is being said and what is being heard, what is being received and what is being revealed.

At the origin of your consciousness, there is a paradox. When you are present for this, you develop a capacity to discern the object of your awareness without being absorbed into the associations that arise out of the awareness. Authentic engagement is an exchange that offers presence to the situation long enough and dynamically enough to pull all involved parties into a state of possibility. Authentic engagement fosters a trajectory toward resolution, which again opens up all parties to new possibilities.

To act and speak without feeling the compulsion to manufacture who you are requires that you *find* yourself in the moment, allowing personal thoughts and feelings to inform your words, behaviors, and actions. To stand in presence requires a willingness to experience and manage your thoughts, physical feelings, behaviors, and emotions in a continued stream of consciousness. As you remain genuinely connected, you also must be vigilantly aligned internally and relationally. This flow of information—*data*—is the dynamic exchange between your inner and outer world, cultivated by an ever-expanding conscious container that allows for the revelation of all that is seeking your attention.

This means that you accept each moment into consciousness by paying attention, allowing yourself to listen to others. You adjust your tempo and intensity to act and react to the life surrounding you. When something *false* is operating, you *authentically* recognize and manage it, even disclose it if necessary. Imagine saying this: "As I am trying to respond to your question, I realize that I am moving away from what I really think. I would rather reframe the conversation and tell you exactly how I feel about this situation."

You must repeatedly and consciously return to your origin, your original authority, and find a means of communication and behavior that will allow you to reside within a sense of personal wholeness. If you can consistently find that authentic place in yourself, others will rest in relationship to you. Authenticity is codetermined; who you are is based on your connections. You do not exist in isolation. Instead, you are interdependent with others, and how you think, feel, and act is the net result of your relational influences.

Many people only have their authentic experience: their pain, their story, their love, their loss. Authenticity allows you to reveal yourself, all at once or little by little. There are moments when we turn away from what is right in front of us. The next time you turn away, turn back into the moment and welcome the unexpected, unanticipated intrusion of something that only moments before was hidden. Remove the wax and find what is waiting.

Your Authenticity Self-Assessment

Instructions: Use the scale below to indicate how each statement applies to you in your work setting. It is important to evaluate the statements honestly and without overthinking your answers.

0 NEVER   **1** RARELY   **2** SOMETIMES   **3** USUALLY

_____ I recognize and share what I am holding onto during conflict situations.

_____ I share my perceived imperfections of myself.

_____ I have empathy for the imperfections I perceive in others.

_____ I avoid saying something is true when I know it is not.

_____ I avoid making agreements I don't intend to keep.

_____ I highlight obstacles that I knowingly place in my way.

_____ I offer counter opinions when I disagree with others.

SCORING: Add up the total number of points from each question.

Score of 0 or 1: *What a perfect opportunity to begin to practice a deeper level of authenticity. If you find yourself rejecting this statement, that is the best place to start.*

Score from 2 to 7: *You might have more work to do to employ the Power of Authenticity in a more consistent manner. This quiz can be the first step in reaching toward a deeper level of authenticity. Look through your answers and make a note of any questions that received a 0 or a 1.*

Score from 8 to 14: *You are finding several opportunities to access the power and have the opportunity to discover more. Look through your coming days and weeks and determine one or two times where you may be able to set an intention to be more authentic in specific situations.*

Score from 15 to 20: *Authenticity is enmeshed in your daily practice. Continue to recognize the benefits of using it where it makes sense for you, for others, and for your relationships.*

Score of 21: *You know and share exactly who you are in the moments that make up this life.*

To access free resources on cultivating the Power of Authenticity, please visit us at www.presentcompany .work or use this QR code.

The Power of Connection

The potential for connection emerges when induction, aware-ness, and authenticity are present. With a conscious deter-mination, these powers cultivate the soil out of which connec-tion can arise.

You build a flowerbed, fill it with soil, seedlings, and just the right amount of fertilizer and water. At this point, you could in-struct your garden to "grow," leaving it to its own devices. Maybe a few plants would survive, growing one way or the other, but would your garden thrive? Would it bear fruit?

With a more intentional and conscious gardening approach, you may determine that the seedlings need frequent watering. So you install a drip system. As your garden takes root and the seeds begin to sprout, weeds, left unattended, could rob the soil of its nutrients. These you judiciously remove. Because you care about the garden, you recognize the need to attend to it regularly. You monitor it and maybe even make plans, based on the pattern of the sun, to shift things for the new growing season. Willing and eager, you make incremental and ongoing adjustments to ensure, to the best of your ability, that you cultivate a bountiful and thriving garden.

There is something else you learn from your garden: it develops and grows through cycles of birth, life, death, and transition. It is attuned to the seasons and subject to the influences of its location, the climate, and your degree of attention. You understand that your garden exists in a context shaped by the recurring cycles of growth, development, and change.

Now, with this metaphor in mind, let's shift our attention to organizations. Organizations thrive because of their culture, and culture is formed and informed by the relational connections of people within it. We don't know how many organizations have the time or the patience to actually cultivate their culture. This would require keeping an eye on long-term success. Many organizations are fixated on short-term results. The success of your efforts depends upon your frame of reference. If you think in the short term, let's say that on a quarter-to-quarter basis, you have a very short season. Without a longer view, tempered with an understanding of the cycles that businesses run through, you may lack the patience and determination to properly design a strategy that includes nurturing the seeds you have sown.

Cultivation suggests preparation and regular maintenance, so that what you have planted can thrive. As part of this conscious determination, you realize that you cultivate your relationships in much the same way you cultivate a garden. Through developing rapport and similar values and interests with your team or colleagues, you prepare the basis that supports the potential to grow and prosper together. This mutual development is the result of connecting through *dialogue*, which is the context where you mutually participate in creating the conditions for connection. Because connection develops through dialogue, you can't do it alone. You can't unilaterally declare that you will be successful. You can, however, have an experience of mutuality when you build the context, the team, and the organization that supports success.

There are organizations that try to set culture through attempting to install some preconceived notion of what a functional culture should look like. There's a question often debated: "Where does the culture begin?" Many people land on the idea that culture is set and developed from the determination of the organization's leadership. Others recognize that sustainable culture develops from the ground up. Either way, attempting to construct a culture by adding a ping-pong table to unused open space, instigating Friday happy hour, or hanging ten principles on the wall has, at best, short-term value. Setting up a culture based on good ideas has a short half-life. Growing a culture based on authentic relational engagement has the potential for an unlimited life span. Maintaining a culture through relational connections disperses the risk of failure. Successful organizations recognize the dynamic impact that multiple, functional relationships have on stability and overall growth.

As a leader or team member, it is important to realize that your lived experience is very different from that of others. What influences your perceptions and your experiences is your locality, gender, economic asymmetries, and social status. Your family heritage, your set of values—these greatly inform your lived experience. As a leader determined to form meaningful connections, how do you stitch this whole thing together? What do you offer that will motivate people to grow their connections with one another?

Cultivating seeds correlates with setting the right conditions for connections to be enriched by individual differences. When employing induction, awareness, and authenticity to every interaction, you increase the likelihood of success. This success is rooted in your relationships. These relationships depend upon the depth of rapport and connection that exists between you and your team members.

This *soil* is the context or ground out of which authentic connection reveals itself. It is a place where the internal is informed by the external, where the self is informed by the other. This ground is a place where a means of exchange exists. We refer to this as the intermediate zone. It is a third area that is rich in potential. For the kind of exchange that builds connection, it is important that a leader does not impose themselves too greatly on the developing process. The leader facilitates their inner thoughts and feelings to resonate by being present and aware and by openly and transparently feeling what is transpiring with others. One set of values and experience does not work against another; they are mutually supportive. One does not defeat the other; both are held in a vibrant tension that brings forth new possibilities. This authentic presence allows individual team members to connect the uniqueness of their inner life with the outer demands of being an integral member of a team.

Present Cultivation

You can think about induction as a process of tilling the soil. It is foundational preparation for authentic connection to emerge. As you prepare the ground of exchange, you first bring your awareness to your context, whether it be a phone call, a one-on-one meeting, a team meeting, or an all-hands. Think in terms of time.

Induction moves all involved into the time zone where the connection is to manifest. Think in terms of the physical space and attend to it so that it supports and does not distract from your meeting. Take a moment to disclose *where you are coming from*. Invite other members to show up in a similar manner by checking in and offering their real-time thoughts, experiences, and feelings. Inductions can be brief and efficient and provide a conscious means for all parties to disclose where they stand psychologically, emotionally, and physically.

As you and others begin to foster the ground of exchange and open up to the possibility of connecting, awareness begins to shift into the present moment. It is in the present moment that the patterns of the past loosen their grip, allowing you to turn your attention to the future and its unforeseen promises. Awareness is that discerning factor that determines what seeds you and others are going to plant, and how you will cultivate the process, so these seeds take root, grow, and bear fruit. It is through this process of cultivation that we are able to codetermine what propagates and influences the outcome of our connections.

Core behaviors: These are the core behaviors of authentic connection: identify the time and space, show up and be present, navigate through any obstacles, deepen your alignment, and repeat. Each connection you have throughout the day runs a cycle: birth–life–death–transition, birth–life–death–transition. That is the cycle of life enacted all day, every day in your personal and professional life.

System under stress: Even the best system is going to break down again and again. This cycle of connection or cycle of life (if you will) does not function in isolation. This cycle is persistently subject to the influence of change. The stress placed on a system is what ensures its relevance and its viability. Stress informs us that change is afoot. As it presses its way into consciousness, stress lets us know that we need to adapt. Stress, from this perspective, is an ally that supports continued growth and development. Not enough stress or tension, and the ground of connection goes fallow, producing less fruit. Too much stress, and the growth of the fruit is stunted.

Encourage life cycles: First, understand that all systems, whether they are incidental connections with colleagues in the hallway or at an offsite, depend on the influence of change. When things fall apart, use your training to pull the process of connection back together. When things are too dense, too congested, and nothing is happening, allow things to breathe, to loosen, to release and relax . . . to slow and fall apart. The core element of all life cycles is breath. It comes in and it goes out. Find your way of accepting a willingness to feel into and through the process of change.

Depth of connection: Going to depth means delving into your thoughts and those of your teammates and remaining present for the feelings you unearth. You accept confusion and meander just long enough to release stored tensions, inculcating new insights and understanding. You don't allow relationships to fracture; but at the same time, you don't jump into fix-it mode. You stick together within yourself and your team, trusting the complex process of facing change. As a leader, as you go to depth, you take your relationships to depth, you take your team to depth. It is here that you move away from your quick and shallow understandings or assumptions. In depth you open to the influences of new possibilities, where you can hold and facilitate process.

Recently, we were scheduled to facilitate a two-hour executive team meeting with a client to begin a process of clarifying the team's—and, by extension, the company's—values. This was intended to inform what changes were necessary for increased success in the new year. A few hours before the meeting, the CEO cancelled, citing something more urgent that needed the team's attention. On the surface, this appeared to be true. Their pricing model was flawed, and a new approach and strategy was necessary to ensure the viability of several pending proposals. However, under the surface, something else was stirring. The CEO had been exhibiting odd behaviors, which we understood to be in direct relationship with the team's newly distributed leadership style. Key decisions were being moved to each department, which required less top-down oversight and management by the CEO. The CEO was unconsciously feeling threatened by these changes. Even though this distribution of leadership was a positive sign of growth, the CEO's unilateral and reactive impulses prompted the cancellation of the team meeting, causing significant obstruction. It would take another month or two for that team to find its way back to the position necessary to clarify their values and set the stage for higher team functionality.

Depth of connection is an inclusive context that allows for a richer and more informed process of dialogue. However, as you deepen into your connection, it can be threatening. Depth of connection is inclusive of all thoughts, feelings, and behaviors, even the unwanted ones. If these insights are held and managed, they can productively inform the developmental process of leadership and teams. However, it is necessary to hold both the process and the intensity of the process and not allow it to fracture.

As you continue to deepen your process of leadership, you will encounter what lies below the surface. The CEO in the example we just described would need to consciously self-reflect to understand what was informing the impulses that prompted him to cancel the meeting. He would need to trust the commitments that established the process. He would have to respect that every team member formed their expectations rooted in the agreements, whether implicit or explicit. Meetings require scheduling, and to commit to being present, significant time, energy, and consideration are necessary. To cancel a meeting is deeply disappointing, expensive, and works to erode the very fibers that have been woven to support a functional team environment. These broken agreements and impulsive influences work to undercut the connections necessary for individual and team success. What is the true cost of the collateral damage incurred by a team when their leader acts unilaterally and without awareness?

Hallmarks of Regenerative Connections

Data flow: Relational data provides information about yourself and about others. How you feel and how others feel is data. What you are thinking and what they are thinking is data. What develops as a result of your dialogue and your being together is data. Your decisions, collaborative processes, and achieved outcomes are all manifestations of data flow. Maintaining this flow is the key to connection. You do not gather data on the basis of *first this event and now that event*. Data flow is based on a process of continuous, self-renewing exchange. It is a mistake to assume that just because you make a connection, the relationship will be sustainable, or that the project will proceed, or that the team will develop. Relationships and the connections within them are living systems that need ongoing care and consideration. This can be achieved and sustained by continuously checking in, questioning, listening, and assessing. Do this even when things are going *well*.

Agreements: Placing expectations on others requires that you tie your expectations directly to agreements. There is an upcoming meeting with the board, and each manager is responsible for preparing a set of slides to make up their section of the board deck. All expectations need to be based on well-formed agreements. If you and someone you thought you had an agreement with fail to keep the agreement, ask yourself, "Did I establish a well-formed agreement?" Agreements have to be simple and clear, and they need to be articulated and agreed upon three times. The when, where, what, and how needs to be included with each iteration.

If you form expectations of yourself, one another, or your clients without considering clear agreements, you are bound to be disappointed. Keep every agreement you make. Make as few agreements as possible. Finally, if you are unable to keep the agreement, renegotiate the agreement with the person with whom you made it. Without the application of mindful awareness, if you are like everyone else, you form numerous agreements on a daily basis that you have no intention of keeping. This oversight becomes fertile ground for disappointment, resentment, and failed relational success.

Empathy: When working with senior management, one quality of leadership emerges as an absolute necessity for successful communication and organizational well-being: empathy. We define empathy as *a capacity to experience the thoughts, feelings, and behaviors of other people, while simultaneously differentiating one's own thoughts, feelings, and behaviors.* This quality or capacity is something many people naturally possess. However, under the stress of running an organization, over long periods of time, necessity often trumps propriety. What is responsible for the successful development of the organization—cooperative effort—is moved to the background, and *efficiency* and *control* in response to the *bottom line* pushes mutual regard into the shadows.

As this occurs, there is a decrease in authentic human connection and communication resulting in diminished empathy. Eventually, a split will emerge, and the fractured parts silo and begin to function independently. Individuals, departments, and teams tend toward functioning in service of their independent objectives, often antithetical to the well-being of other departments and the organization.

The devolution of an organization can be successfully corrected, as empathy is reestablished and cultivated as a conscious antidote to this dysfunctional process.

Connection as Ceremony

You have signals in your body that relay when you are deeply connecting with another person, group, or the natural world. These moments tell you, in a rather dramatic way, that you are a part of something greater than yourself. The ceremonial practice of placing yourself inside a context beyond your control supports the cultivation of a culture of connection.

Ceremony holds and is determined by reciprocal states of engagement, a collective joining: playing music, dancing, singing, eating. When reciprocally engaged, you may experience a kind of buzzing or tingling in the upper back, between the shoulder blades and into the neck, often accompanied by a slight sweating, a chill, or even goosebumps. It is a radiating, very immediate experience of energy flow. These bodily sensations signal situational engagement and ground you in the present moment. When connections happen authentically and naturally, we can train ourselves to be present.

Managing through Disconnection

What do you typically experience when you are with other people, at home, in your teams or groups? Are people paying attention to you, to one another, to themselves? Are they open to connection? How present are they? Do they examine their motivations before they act? When you interact with others, are you open, kind, and considerate? Do you intentionally think about how you can contribute to deepening your rapport with others?

The demands of the day can prevent you from knowing what you think or feel in any given moment. As a matter of fact, too much thinking or feeling can work against your ability to act. Too little thinking or feeling, and your actions function outside of authentic connection. Daily life can make you feel as though you are being swept from one moment to the next without a second to reflect. We might even suggest that this is *normal*. Being swept along and unable to tether yourself to that which is happening right in front of you can leave you feeling as if you are outside of your control: life is happening *to* you and without your consent. Living too many of this kind of day, back to back, supports an imbalance that becomes the root cause of neurosis, stressed-out relationships, and a life based on challenges, not choice.

The cultivation of connection is like the cultivation of a garden with one major difference: the life cycle of a relationship unfolds from moment to moment, but the life cycle of a garden happens over the span of an entire year.

Incidental, normalized interactions that maintain the appearance of connection are a natural sorting of positioning and proximity that seem to work, to some degree, for a while. You know one another at this introductory level, and that's just fine; you like being around one another, perhaps. You collaborate in maintaining this comfort zone. Through intention or through circumstance, you continue to assemble. Perhaps you do so without the understanding that at some point you're going to have to cultivate these relationships to keep them growing. Like anything that is alive, you may have to open up more ground, take a few risks, reach out into the unknown, so that light can shine onto latent possibilities. Soon enough, you may be called on to participate in the unfolding nature of change. Are you consciously preparing yourself?

Reversing Course

How do you manage through cycles of disconnection? How do you become aware that things are heading in the wrong direction? Can you reverse or correct the dynamics to bring yourself and others back to alignment? The primary hallmark of disconnection is revealed in moments when things *don't make sense*. A tell-tale sign is when process is disrupted and resistance and friction appear. Simply put, the situation that you are a part of becomes increasingly uncomfortable. This is an indication—an early warning signal, if you will—that change is afoot, and the predominant process is attempting to evolve. Some things are not sitting right in the room, and they need to be addressed so that the process can continue and the system can evolve. If you ignore this human element, pulling yourself together and marching on with a directive, you are sowing seeds of disconnection. It is likely that even though you continue your efforts to grow the connections, without understanding the human element that is calling for your attention, you are likely to fail. Connection is trilateral, dependent on all parties: you, others, and the relationships that make up the team. Make an effort to move through the obstacles. Trust the process and find your way back connection. Things will make sense if you let them.

Your fundamental connection with one another is a preexisting, innate condition that has the potential to become a reality when one person's consciousness joins the consciousness of another. Connection is that medium of exchange necessary for couples, families, and teams to function successfully. We succeed because we work together and recognize our oneness. This is most noticeable when we look at sports teams. A team is not a collection of individuals. A team is the result of individuals moving out of their comfort zones and, in a very real sense, transmuting themselves as a part of something that is far greater. The subset of team culture rests in the dynamics of all existing relationships. Teams are a collection of relationships, not individuals. If you develop and grow your relationships with other team members, you participate in growing the team.

Can You Hear Me Now?

Problematic connections make you less effective in your determined pursuit. This is when you know your connection is a problem:

Connection is assumed and not negotiated: When things happen too quickly, pay attention. Ask yourself, *Did the person you are with enlist you into a relational dynamic that dramatically shifts you from where you were to where they want you to be? Are they taking you for a ride?* Relationship is built on a give-and-take over time. It takes time and multiple interactions to establish an authentic connection with someone.

Connection is indigestible: After you have disengaged from the situation or person, you spend too much time replaying the tape of the interaction in your mind. Or you come away with a feeling that is unwanted and difficult to get rid of. You find that you need to share this exchange with someone you trust, in an attempt to make sense of it.

Connection doesn't make sense: If you have difficulty making sense of your experience with the person or situation, it could be because what is occurring doesn't make sense.

Connection disrupts the flow of your work: Someone dropping by to follow up on something, to ask a quick question, to take advantage of your open-door policy should enhance your productivity, not diminish it. This type of disruptive engagement is too expensive. Meetings, particularly scheduled meetings, are the right context to address this type of concern.

Cycles of Growth

Growth depends on deeper soil and more fertilizer spread by your ability to offer greater attention. As a leader, you have to dig deeper and examine the roots to understand what influences the flow and growth of your relationships. You have to move through the inevitable challenges on a regular basis (this is the cultivation piece). To do this, you have to be willing to grow and change and even transform what is happening in this very moment. Growth, change, development, and transformation always happen *now*. This cycle is not going to occur somewhere off in the future. Your opportunity is available in every interaction, within every relationship.

Growth, change, and transformation can be uncomfortable. Through design or circumstance, development is disruptive. What works for you today can actually limit you tomorrow, if it is resistant to change. You have a golf swing, and you continue to play golf in the same way you've always played. You hold your racket the same way, every time, as a tennis ball sails toward you. It is the same routine, whether you head into the gym or lace your shoes for a run. Yet, one day you realize that there is a problem. The ball is not going where you expect it to go, your performance at the gym is routine and you are losing interest in it, you suffer an injury even though you followed the same warm-up routine.

To get back to where you want to be, you have to come here, to this present moment. It is in this moment that you can begin to untangle. You will have to repattern your swing, and to do that, you must face change. You have to examine how you anticipate your swing and the steadiness of your breathing. What posture is your body adopting? Are the muscles too tense? Are you distracted? Is there something you should examine? Should you change what you are focusing on? Should you direct your awareness and mind in some other way? These considerations are part of a very dynamic, yet disruptive, process one must experience to recover or achieve a better golf swing. You have to disrupt, disrupt even what is working, long enough to improve. Naturally, like most of us, you may be reluctant to risk experiencing the disruptive nature of change, particularly in your relationships, teams, and businesses.

To allow the disruption of change, you may risk being somewhat of a mess. You may risk being a little too obvious to yourself, and you might imagine you are also a little too visible to others. Consciousness of yourself in the moment can be annoying. When you reveal things about yourself that are not *fully baked*, you can never be sure how it is going to play out. As you show your vulnerabilities, you face the possibility of projected biases. You may seek cover and retreat to the comfort of the familiar: avoiding eye contact, distractedly attending to your devices, relying on distance or marginal participation to pull you out of the light of exposure. Rather than risking the vulnerabilities of change, you find yourself covering up and disappearing into the shadows. However, these patterns of protection tee up a potential problem. As you and those around you divert yourselves from the opportunity to engage and make improvements, inadvertently and incrementally you participate in unconsciously choosing to wait until you no longer have a choice.

The Unexamined Life

How often do any of us have the time or inclination to stop long enough to reflect? This unconscious patterning leaves many, many parts of yourself unintegrated. As you forfeit the opportunity to fully actualize yourself, this potential is put on hold or buried. At some point, the unexamined life or the life on hold, the buried life, begins to call for your attention. It is the call of the soul; and if it is not addressed directly, it can disrupt your existence and sabotage the evolution of your relationships. You can look at this in terms of a marriage. If you put too much on hold, at some point you're going to be called to deal with it. The slow erosion of trust occurs when disappointments go unresolved. Over time, not showing up on time chips away at the foundation of your relationship. You ask your child to wait and wait and wait. At some point, their capacity for waiting is going to extinguish, and you're going to have some kind of collision. Children will form bonds just as solidly with your absence as they will with your presence. They know you because of how you show up in their life. They know you equally well when you predictably disappoint them. A teammate knows who you are. They spend more hours a day in relationship with you than does your family. The key to successful relationships rests in your willingness to self-examine and take every opportunity to listen to what is seeking to reveal itself. Your relationships make up who you are. Your soul reveals itself as it deepens and broadens all of your connections.

When you begin to disconnect from your family, from your body, from your hopes and dreams, something is being left behind. It is time to pause a moment, reflect, and develop a strategy for recovery. Is there a difference in how you think, feel, and behave when you connect deeply and authentically? Do you actually know to what degree you are connected with someone and they to you? You might even wonder about the degree to which you inhabit the same reality as the person you are with. You may wonder if there is such a thing as a joint world in common and the degree to which you coinhabit such a world.

When we think of teams, we wonder about the degree of presence of the members. Presence requires a capacity that has to be elastic enough to allow for unexpected change. A shift in how you feel can impact your presence. Maybe a positive response enhances your willingness and ability to bring people into a more connected state. A negative response may cause you to detach, pull back, and retreat from the moment, as it fosters your inadvertent participation in disconnection.

Presence emerges for the individual, the couple, the family or the team, when all four powers exist in equal measure. Culture emerges as transitions inform a flow of unfolding continuity. **Induction** sets the stage or creates the context. **Awareness** prepares this context and regulates its capacity to receive what is seeking to emerge. **Authenticity** is a persistent state of differentiation, where the obstacles that cloud clarity are addressed in this moment and inform the following moment. **Connection** is that third thing that emerges between you and other forms of life ensuring an exchange of thoughts, feelings, emotions, behaviors, and energy. In a flow of continuity, Induction + Awareness + Authenticity + Connection = Presence.

To access free resources on cultivating the Power of Connection, please visit us at www.presentcompany .work or use this QR code.

Present Company

The Four Powers of Presence establish a cultivated ecosystem, a Culture of Presence. **Induction** primes the moment, allowing for personal and interpersonal **awareness**. In turn, as you shift outside of familiar patterning, there is a possibility of becoming more open, naturally more inclusive, and, for the sake of **authenticity**, vulnerable. Your openness creates the right environment for bona fide bilateral **connections** to form. These connections then ensure that you are available for sustainable **continuity**. As you transition and openly greet the opportunity embedded in the next moment, this regenerative cycle is primed to continue.

When there is continuity, the start of each new cycle of presence begins from the apex of the previous cycle. The leader, if *present*, has the potential to step into the team at the exact location she left the previous meeting. Each previous cycle is fertile ground for continued growth. And each cycle prepares ground for the next. Once cultivated, a culture of presence becomes regenerative.

Circularity, cycles, beginnings, middles and ends, transitions.

What comes around goes around. One hallmark of presence is this series of continued, self-renewing engagements. There is a turning in to the moment with a depth of consciousness that works to foster a sustainable and present culture. Culture emerges as the regenerative ecosystem that in turn supports this process. In any given moment, a leader has a choice to serve or work against sustainability and regeneration. The Four Powers provide the necessary tools to support this sustained creative, productive, and self-renewing action.

When the Four Powers converge, the presence is a powerful dynamic. Putting them all together is what is important. Once done, continuing to do so may be a challenge. The key is sensitizing yourself to what it looks or feels like when one of the powers is left out of consciousness. What follows is a chart highlighting the unintended results that can occur when one or more of the powers may be missing.

The Continuity Chart

Induction + Awareness + Authenticity + Connection = **Presence**

~~Induction~~ + Awareness + Authenticity + Connection = **Limited Sustainability**

Induction + ~~Awareness~~ + Authenticity + Connection = **Diminished Potential**

Induction + Awareness + ~~Authenticity~~ + Connection = **False Outcomes**

Induction + Awareness + Authenticity + ~~Connection~~ = **Aborted Progress**

Presence

Induction + Awareness + Authenticity + Connection

= **Presence**

When the Four Powers are in residence, your ability to stay present is greatly enhanced. As you transition from one moment to the next, the continuity of your interactions fosters the very architecture of a culture of presence.

The lights go down, the show begins. You take that breath and prime yourself for what is about to happen next. The music starts and you shift your awareness to the sound of the drum roll, and when the bass kicks in, you can feel it. You let go and start to groove to the beat, not caring what people may think of your closed eyes and hung head swaying, as the energy washes over you. One song leads to the next, and you feel connected, at one with each moment.

The street ends and the path through the forest is marked. You take a moment to witness the transition between pavement and dirt. You become aware of the slight cooling in the air, the deep green of the moss-covered trees, the uneven nature of the path. You are open to hearing the sounds of a squirrel running up a tree, a bird calling in the distance, your breath quickening and then deepening as you head further into the canopy. You stop trying to control and just allow for what may next present itself, whether it is something you see, hear, or feel. The rest of the walk seems to flow seamlessly, leaving you with a sense of calming awe.

Limited Sustainability

~~Induction~~ + Awareness + Authenticity + Connection
= **Limited Sustainability**

Without maintaining cycles that include Induction, you inadvertently foster limited relational sustainability. Without Induction, there is no guarantee that you or those you engage with are able to transition unencumbered from your previous encounters. This missed opportunity may result in perpetuating cycles that are not self-renewing or sustainable.

You arrive at the meeting and everyone is looking at their devices, so you do the same. We are all busy and need to get work done, and the meeting is just another one on a calendar that is filled with events requiring your attendance. The person who called the meeting walks in seven minutes late and begins to talk. They don't check in, address their tardiness, or in any way acknowledge the moment. They have done nothing to induce the team to show up and connect. Any connections that may occur will be severely limited, leaving people isolated and looking through their own lenses instead of through a collective one.

Diminished Potential

Induction + ~~Awareness~~ + Authenticity + Connection
= **Diminished Potential**

With the absence of awareness, growth will be stalled, both within yourself and within your relationships and team. By not being attuned empathically, you inadvertently create a one-sided vision, limiting the potential for growth.

The team leader enters the room and looks around to each person in the circle. What unfolds is a monologue, speaking *at* versus speaking *with* the group. While filled with vulnerability and authenticity, he lacks awareness of his impact. He is knowledgeable, speaking clearly, but he is not engaging his audience. Due to the lack of inclusivity put forth by the speaker, when he is finished, connections may have been established but the potential for future growth is severely diminished.

False Outcomes

Induction + Awareness + ~~Authenticity~~ + Connection
= **False Outcomes**

False outcomes foster a climate that, over time, normalizes corrupted deliverables. You will see this when agreements are not kept, when expectations end in disappointment, when behaviors are in service of something hidden and do not deliver growth.

The team unites and sets an intention for the day. Team members check in to align the desired impact. They set their intentions with one another and the team as a whole. The day progresses with discussion, debate, and a series of agreements and commitments. The day ends, but when the team returns to work over the next few days, it is evident that they didn't all commit to what was agreed upon. When the opportunity to examine doubts, voice concerns, and risk showing vulnerability presented itself, not everyone spoke up. This lack of authenticity fostered a process that resulted in desired outcomes not being met and expected results falling short.

Aborted Progress

Induction + Awareness + Authenticity + ~~Connection~~

= **Aborted Progress**

Without a connection between yourself and the others within a family, group, or team, progress can be derailed. Although the three other powers have been activated, if not nurtured, the cultivated ecosystem will struggle to fully develop. The connections will fray, as they have been incorrectly assumed and not mutually negotiated. The result is a garden that, while mindfully cultivated, primed, and encouraged to bear fruit, is left sorely unattended, overgrown with weeds and forgotten.

The Container of High Performance

True high-performing teams do not just achieve the goal and stop. They continue to improve by recognizing what they have done well. This happens even amid unexpected setbacks, bouts of poor performance, and bad decision-making. They look to answer and take action instead of waiting for someone else to take control. They own challenging situations rather than blaming them on others. They speak up, not taking cover and waiting it out. They work to sustain the results they have achieved by nurturing the connections that have been created. These connections result in a cultivated culture of high performance.

Over the years we have witnessed teams and leaders achieving various levels of high performance. One of the things that these teams and individuals have in common is their willingness to recognize that the dynamics in the team can be adjusted to encourage immediacy of participation.

This recognition includes the ability to do the following:

» Flatten the social status of everyone in the room, so all voices have equal value.

» Share expectations, so that people will risk being more intimate and revealing.

» Reduce false and unnecessary policies and procedures.

» Banish the dynamics that knowingly support bias, favoritism, and passive-aggressiveness.

» Focus on the dynamics that remain. Support connection, kindness, growth, and change.

» Honor agreements that have been made, no matter how seemingly small or insignificant.

Systems Under Stress

A hallmark of high performance is revealed under stress. Life doesn't always follow along the expected trajectory the way most of us hope. The unexpected—challenging for individuals and teams—forces them to face the limitations of control. Adversity actually functions as a barometer to measure the strength of resolve.

Stress gives a team the opportunity to see where and how the cracks reveal themselves, allowing all involved to see what needs attention. The goal of a high-performing culture is not to avoid cracks, but to consistently pivot toward what is calling for its attention. Only then, can the culture consciously address and calibrate the situation at hand.

Stressful challenges very often cause a flight, fight, or freeze response, thrusting the culture into survival mode. Teams, when under too much stress, will naturally return to a regressive default position. This is particularly true when global influences directly affect the organization.

In these times, high-performing teams put an extra emphasis on utilizing the Four Powers of Presence. Over the past few months, as this book is being finalized during the onset of the COVID-19 pandemic, organizations have had to transition their entire workforce to a working-from-home platform. Many are faced with drastic drops in sales, as well as layoffs and questions about the company's fiscal future. High stress, countless unknowns, exhausted team members, and a strong undercurrent of uncertainty cause each individual to unconsciously displace their fears onto the team. There is a drive to find solutions, make as many decisions as possible, and keep heads down to carry on. Some of the by-products of these behaviors are miscommunication, inefficiency, building resentments, and missed opportunities.

In trying times, high-performing teams redouble their efforts to connect authentically and maintain the Present Company that they have worked so hard to build.

Once Present Company is established, the goal shifts to sustainability and regeneration. This continuity is rooted in how we handle the transitions, even in the most difficult times, that fill our days and make up our lives. For leaders, we find these transitions to be the greatest challenge. If present transitioning is disallowed, every previous encounter is carried forward to the next. Without presence, when under stress, problems at an organization can cascade and become widespread. When panic sets in, there is little transition time from one moment or activity to the next. This lack of transitional time and space creates an unintended impact on family, friends, partners, colleagues, customers, clients, and communities. Engaging in present transitions ensures that the next opportunity for induction is primed, allowing the cycle of presence to flow.

This flow of information—*data*—is the dynamic exchange

between your inner and outer world, informing a consciousness that allows for the revelation of all that is seeking your attention.

The world is shrinking, and the space we occupy is increasingly subject to dwindling resources. This is not a problem without solutions but rather an opportunity to practice presence. The memory of yesterday can spark the opportunity for today. But the memory of yesterday alone is not enough. Once Present Company is achieved, the connections we have made and the experiences we have had often linger. There is a residue that presents itself in the form of thoughts, feelings, even smells and tastes. When we once again engage, this residue alone cannot be relied on to continue the cycle of presence. We have to be mindful of making consistent inductions, sparking awareness, and demanding authenticity, so the resulting connections run strongly and deeply. This will allow for a cultivated culture to emerge, an intentional and conscious involvement between its people, a shared experience repeated in present time.

Thank you for your presence, and we wish you the power to gift it to others.

Tim and Michael
www.presentcompany.work

Bibliography

Broadwell, Martin M. "Teaching for Learning (XVI.)." *The Gospel Guardian* 20, no. 41 (20 February 20, 1969): 1–3a.

Burger, Mark. *Falling Awake*. Self-published, Lulu Publishing Services, 2015.

About the Authors

Michael Landers, MA, is the founder and president of Culture Crossing Inc., a global consulting company dedicated to finding innovative solutions for groups and individuals working in the multicultural marketplace. Over the past twenty years, Michael has worked with global executives and teams from leading organizations to build essential skills in arenas such as global leadership, coaching, cross-cultural communication, sales and customer service excellence, sustained employee engagement, and cultural diversity and inclusion. His workshops, seminars, and speaking events have drawn more than seventy thousand people on five continents. Although American, Michael was raised in Colombia, Brazil, and the Dominican Republic. Fluent in Spanish and Brazilian Portuguese, proficient in Japanese and Italian, he is the author of the best-selling book *Culture Crossing*, the essential primer to working, living, and thriving in today's increasingly multicultural marketplace and communities. Learn more at www.culturecrossing.net.

Timothy Dukes, PhD, is a veteran psychotherapist, leadership adviser, and father. His expertise in creating and holding a transformational process instills Presence in Leadership for the individual, partnership, family, team, and organization. Tim consults in a variety of institutional settings, working with established business leaders, political visionaries, and emerging innovators. His unique program for individual and organizational development—distilled from thirty years of clinical work, academic research, and contemplative practice—resolves contradiction and opposition through a clarity-based evolutionary practice. His book *The Present Parent Handbook* speaks to his work with families. Learn more at www.drtimothydukes.com.

ELEVATE HUMANITY THROUGH BUSINESS.

Conscious Capitalism, Inc., supports a global community of business leaders dedicated to elevating humanity through business via their demonstration of purpose beyond profit, the cultivation of conscious leadership and culture throughout their entire ecosystem, and their focus on long-termism by prioritizing stakeholder orientation instead of shareholder primacy. We provide mid-market executives with innovative learning exchanges, transformational storytelling training, and inspiring conference experiences all designed to level-up their business operations and collectively demonstrate capitalism as a powerful force for good when practiced consciously.

We invite you, either as an individual or as a business, to join us and contribute your voice. Learn more about the global movement at www.consciouscapitalism.org.

CONSCIOUS CAPITALISM®